MW01630571

Bible Verses for Children

ILLUSTRATED BY Robert S. Jones
EDITED BY Daphna Flegal
COPYEDITED BY Betsi H. Smith

Abingdon Press

Nashville

Sign and Say Bible Verses for Children

Sign, Say, and Remember

Children remember more easily what they learn when you involve both their bodies and their minds—and we want them to remember Bible verses! *Sign and Say Bible Verses for Children* will help your children learn Bible verses using the hand motions of American Sign Language. Use the simple steps listed below to learn these verses yourself and then teach the verses to your children.

- Look at the illustrations.
- Read the written directions.
- Practice, practice, practice! (You need to be able to sign the verse for the children without looking at the page.)

Thank you to Bob Geldreich and Peggy Jennings for their help with signing.

A B C D E F
G H I J K
L M N O P
Q R S T U
V W X Y Z
4

Contents

Good news words

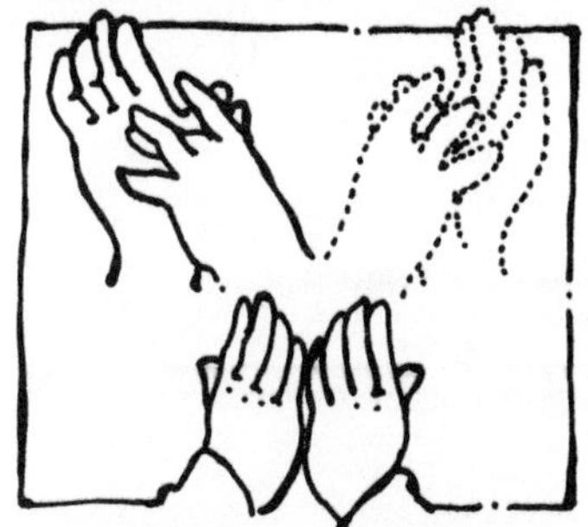

God said, "I will be with you."

Exodus 3:12, adapted

BIBLE VERSE:

God — Point the index finger of your right hand, with the other fingers curled down. Bring the hand down and open the palm.

I — Hold up little finger, with the other fingers curled down. Place at chest.

With — Hold both hands in fists, with thumbs on the outside. Place the fists together, palms touching.

You — Point out with your index finger.

7

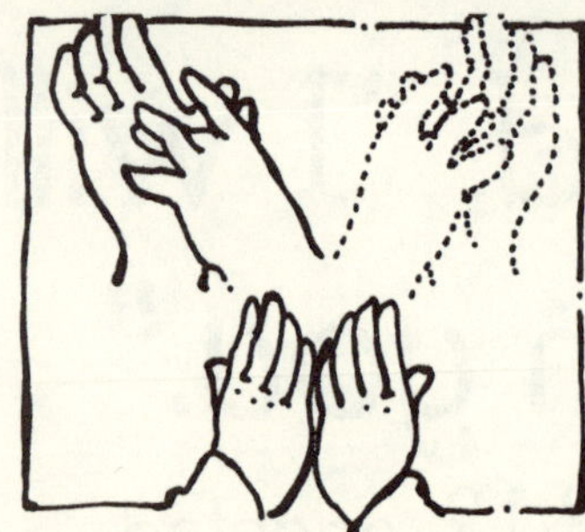

You shall love the LORD your God with all your heart, and with all your soul, and with all your might.

Deuteronomy 6:5

You — Point out with your index finger.

Shall — Place your hand at cheek level, with the palm facing your cheek. Move hand forward.

Love — Cross hands at wrist and press over heart.

8

Lord — Make an "L" with the right hand. Place the "L" at the left shoulder and then move across the body to the right waist.

God — Point the index finger of your right hand, with the other fingers curled down. Bring the hand down and open the palm.

All — Hold the left palm toward the body. Circle right hand out and around the left palm. End with the back of the right hand in the open left hand.

Heart — Draw an outline of a heart on the chest using index fingers.

Soul — Make an "O" with the left hand and place the hand close to the body. Touch the index finger to your thumb on the right hand. Place the right hand into the "O" of the left hand and then move right hand up.

Might — Place both fists over the right side of your chest. Move fists out.

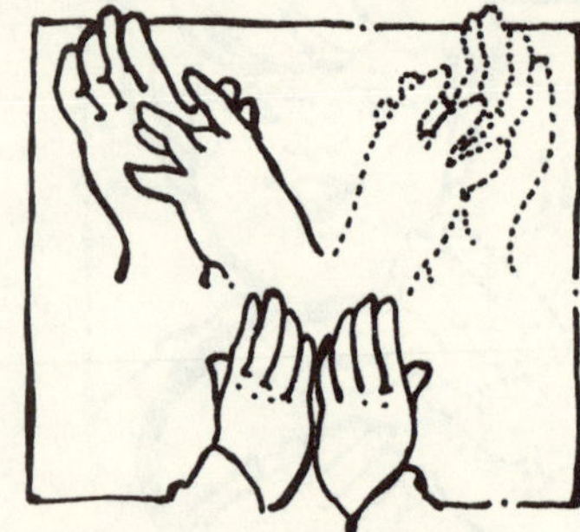

The LORD looks on the heart.

1 Samuel 16:7

BIBLE VERSE:

Lord — Make an "L" with the right hand. Place the "L" at the left shoulder and then move across the body to the right waist.

Look — Make a "V" with one hand. Place the "V" in front of the face, with the palm facing the face. Turn the "V" out so that the palm faces away from the face.

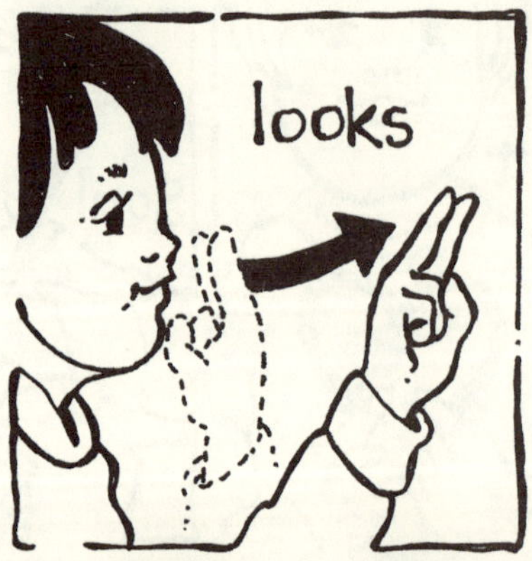

Heart — Draw an outline of a heart on the chest using index fingers.

10

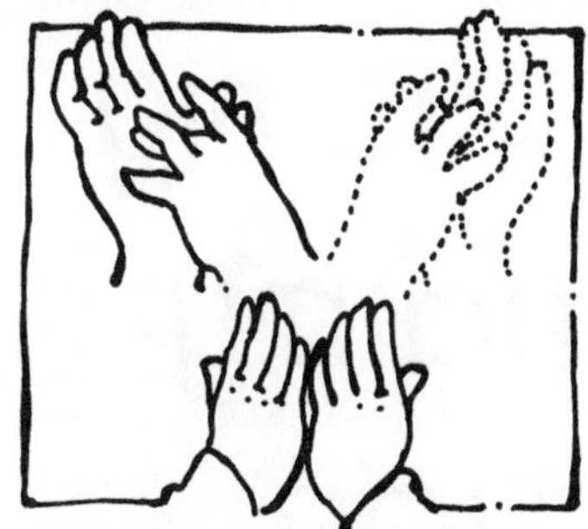

BIBLE VERSE:

The LORD is my shepherd.

Psalm 23:1

Lord — Make an "L" with the right hand. Place the "L" at the left shoulder and then move across the body to the right waist.

My — Open palm and place it on your chest.

Shepherd — Hold the left arm out. Place the right hand palm up on the left arm and make a cutting motion with the right fingers.

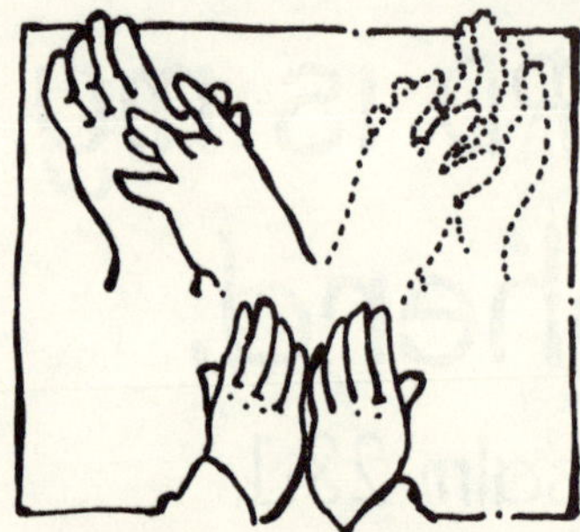

The LORD is my light and my salvation.

Psalm 27:1

LORD — Make an "L" with the right hand. Place the "L" at the left shoulder and then move across the body to the right waist.

My — Open palm and place it on your chest.

Light — Bring both hands in front of body, with the fingertips touching the thumbs. Move the hands up and apart in front of each shoulder. Open hands and spread fingers apart as you move.

Salvation — Make fists with both hands, thumbs out. Cross hands at wrists. Turn fists forward and apart.

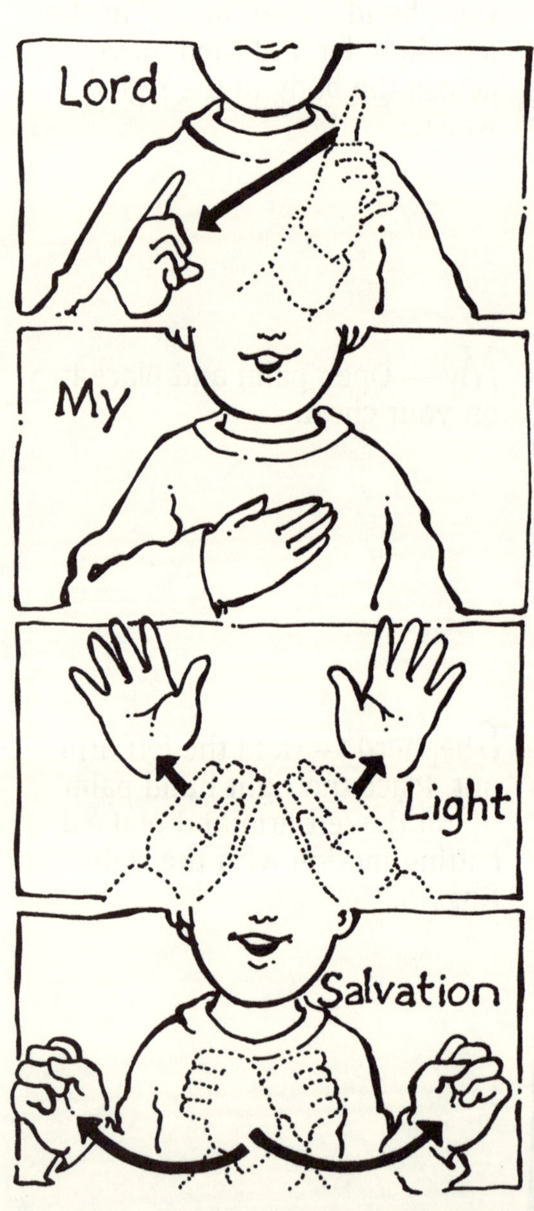

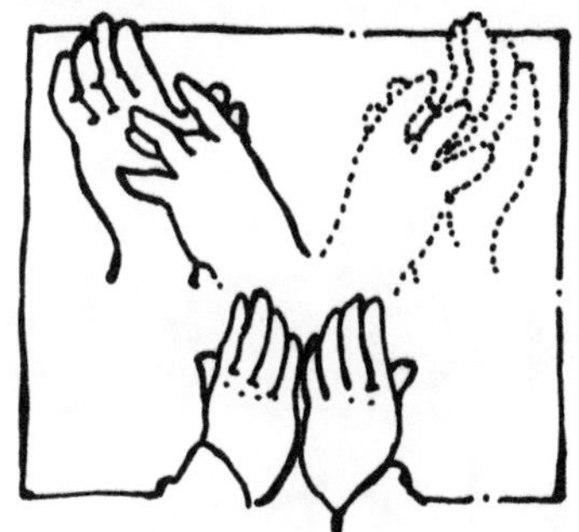

Trust in the LORD.

Psalm 37:3

Trust — Make fists with both hands, thumbs out. Bring both fists to the left of your head. Have your right fist slightly below the left fist.

Lord — Make an "L" with the right hand. Place the "L" at the left shoulder and then move across the body to the right waist.

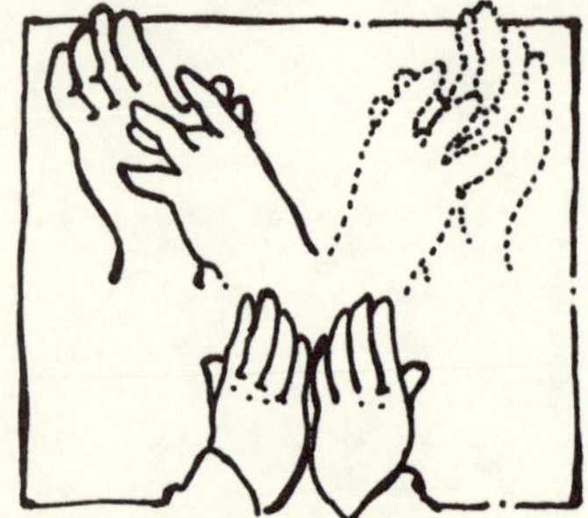

BIBLE VERSE:

Make a joyful noise to the LORD.

Psalm 100:1

Make — Make fists with both hands, thumbs out. Place the right fist on top of the left fist. Turn your fists so that the palms are facing your body. Touch the fists together again.

Joyful — Open both hands, with palms facing toward the chest. Pat the chest several times while moving the hands upward.

Noise — Touch the bottom of the ear with your index finger. Open both hands palms down, with fingers spread apart. Have the right palm behind the left palm. Move the hands toward the left.

LORD — Make an "L" with the right hand. Place the "L" at the left shoulder and then move across the body to the right waist.

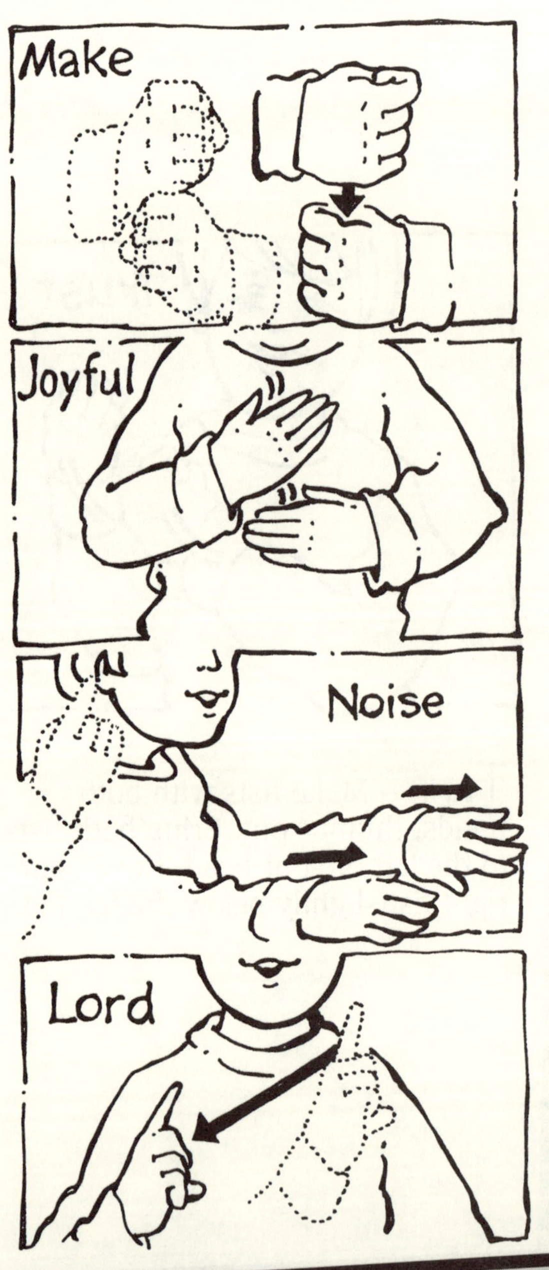

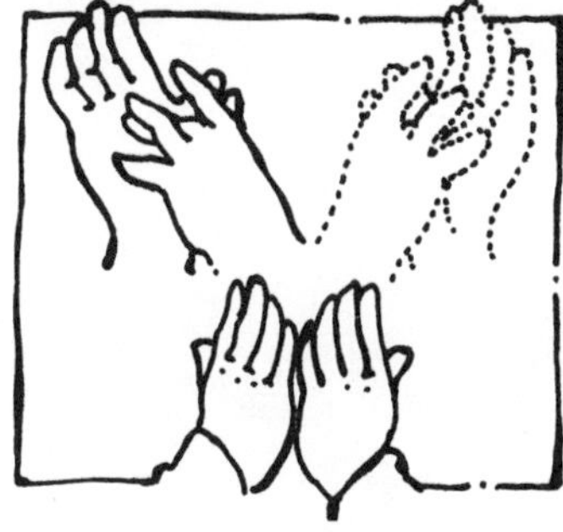

Sing praise to the LORD.

Psalm 105:2, adapted

Sing — Hold the left hand out. Point the fingers of the right hand toward the left palm. Wave the fingertips back and forth over the left palm.

Praise — Clap your hands several times.

Lord — Make an "L" with the right hand. Place the "L" at the left shoulder and then move across the body to the right waist.

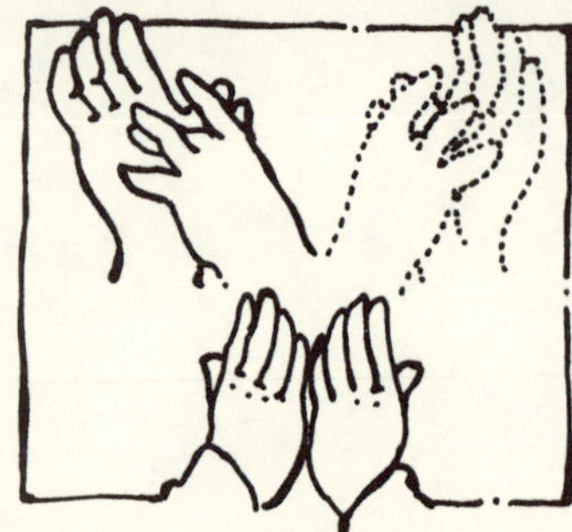

I was glad when they said to me, "Let us go to the house of the LORD!"

Psalm 122:1

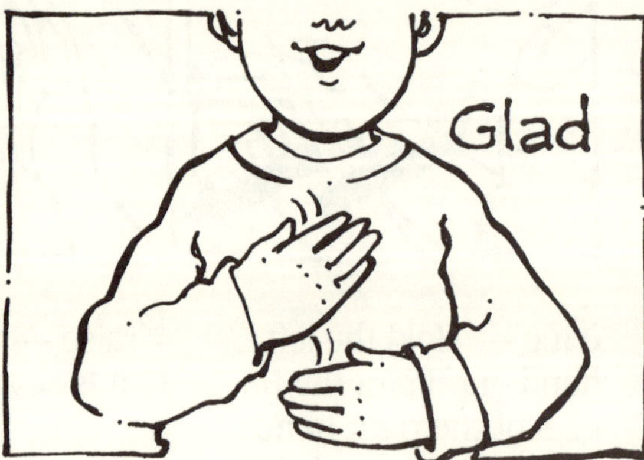

I — Hold up little finger, with the other fingers curled down. Place at chest.

Glad — Open both hands, with palms facing toward the chest. Pat the chest several times while moving the hands upward.

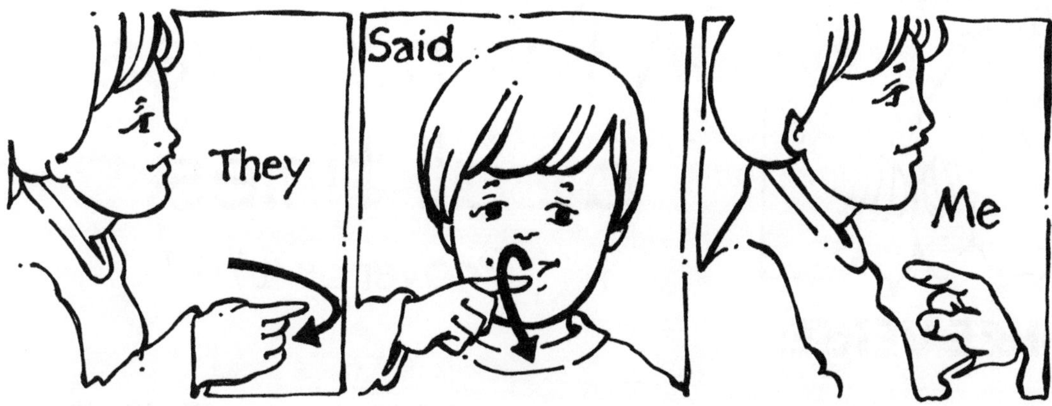

They — Point index finger forward and then move it to the right.

Said — Point right index finger. Hold finger in front of mouth and roll it forward.

Me — Point index finger of the right hand toward your chest.

Go — Point the index fingers of both hands, with one hand slightly behind the other. Move hands forward.

House — Touch the fingertips of both hands together. Bring hands apart and down to outline the roof of a house.

Lord — Make an "L" with the right hand. Place the "L" at the left shoulder and then move across the body to the right waist.

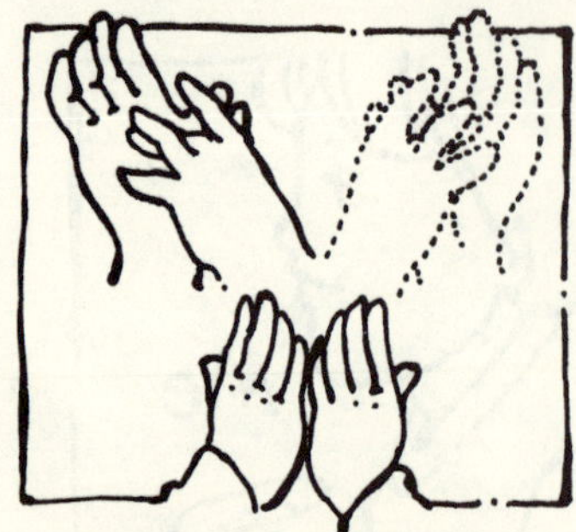

A friend loves at all times.

Proverbs 17:17

BIBLE VERSE:

Friend — Hook the right index finger over the left index finger. Reverse.

Loves — Cross hands at wrist and press over your heart.

All — Hold the left palm toward the body. Circle the right hand out and around the left palm. End with the back of the right hand in the open left hand.

Times — Tap the back of the left hand with the right index finger.

18

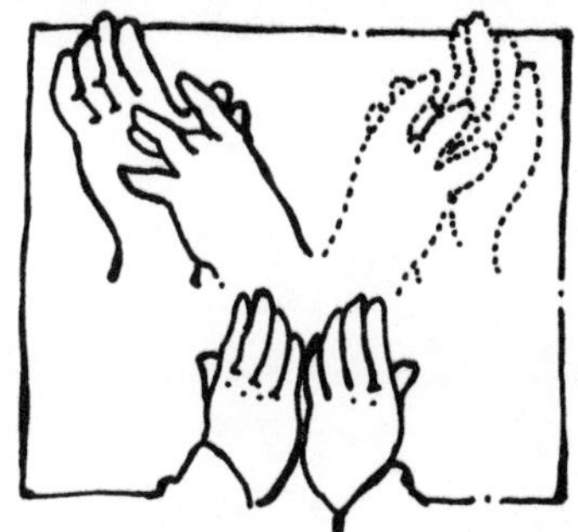

For a child has been born for us.

Isaiah 9:6

Child — Place arms like holding a baby. Rock.

Born — Put the back of the right hand in the palm of the left hand. Move both hands forward and up.

Us — Touch your right shoulder with your index finger. Circle the finger out and then touch the finger to your left shoulder.

19

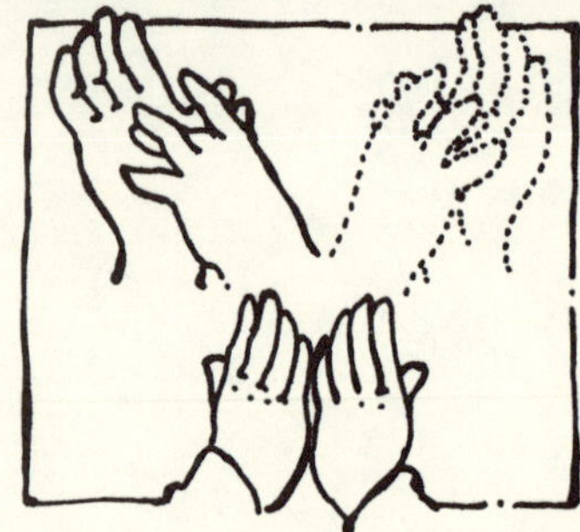

Blessed are the peacemakers, for they will be called children of God.

Matthew 5:9

Blessed — Make a fist with both hands, thumbs out. Place both fists at the mouth. Bring hands forward and down, opening hands with palms down.

Peacemakers — Place the right palm on top of the left palm. Turn hands so that the left palm is on top of the right palm. Move both palms down and to the sides.

Hold hands open, with the palms facing each other in front of your body. Move both hands down.

They — Point index finger forward and then move it to the right.

Will — Place your hand at cheek level, with the palm facing your cheek. Move hand forward.

Called — Extend first two fingers of both hands. Place the fingers of the right hand across the fingers of the left hand, forming an X. Move hands slightly up and forward, then down.

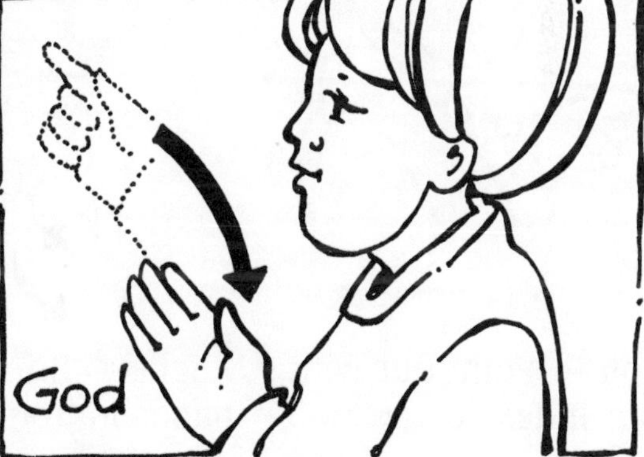

Children — Hold one hand palm down. Pretend to pat the head of a child. Repeat several times.

God — Point the index finger of your right hand, with the other fingers curled down. Bring the hand down and open the palm.

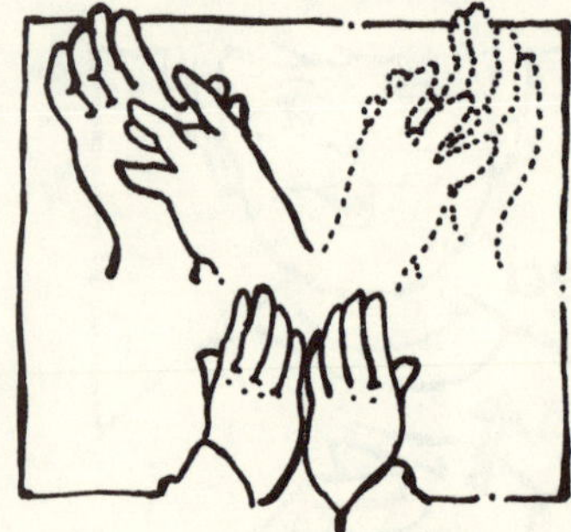

BIBLE VERSE:

You are the light of the world.

Matthew 5:14

© 1997 Abingdon Press

You — Point out with your index finger.

Light — Bring both hands in front of body, with the fingertips touching the thumbs. Move the hands up and apart in front of each shoulder. Open hands and spread fingers apart as you move.

World — Hold out three fingers on each hand (like a W). Circle the right hand around the left hand and place the side of the right hand on the thumb of the left hand.

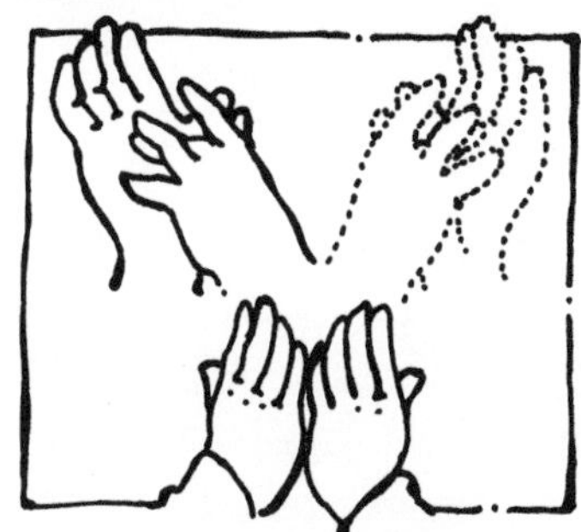

BIBLE VERSE:

Give us this day our daily bread.
Matthew 6:11

Give — Touch thumb and fingertips on each hand. Have hands facing palm down. Turn hands palms up and flatten hands.

Us — Touch your right shoulder with your index finger. Circle the finger out and then touch the finger to your left shoulder.

Day — Extend the index finger of the right hand. Place the right elbow at the left index finger. Move the right index finger in an arc until it touches the inside of the left elbow.

Daily — Make a fist with the thumb out. Rub the fist from the cheek to the chin several times.

Bread — Hold the left hand in front of the body. Move the little finger side of the right hand across the left hand as if slicing bread.

23

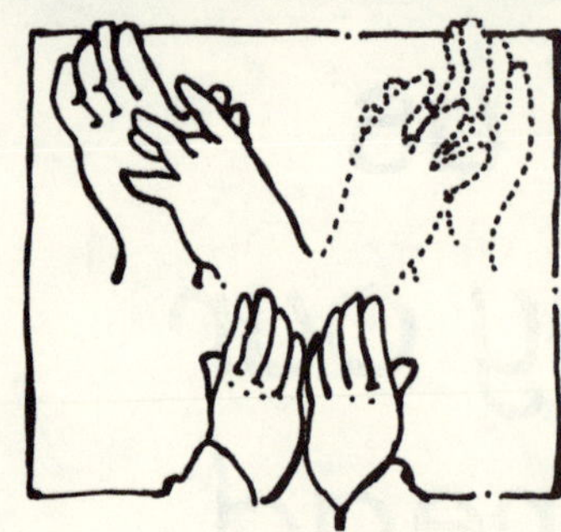

Ask, and it will be given you; search, and you will find; knock, and the door will be opened for you.

Matthew 7:7

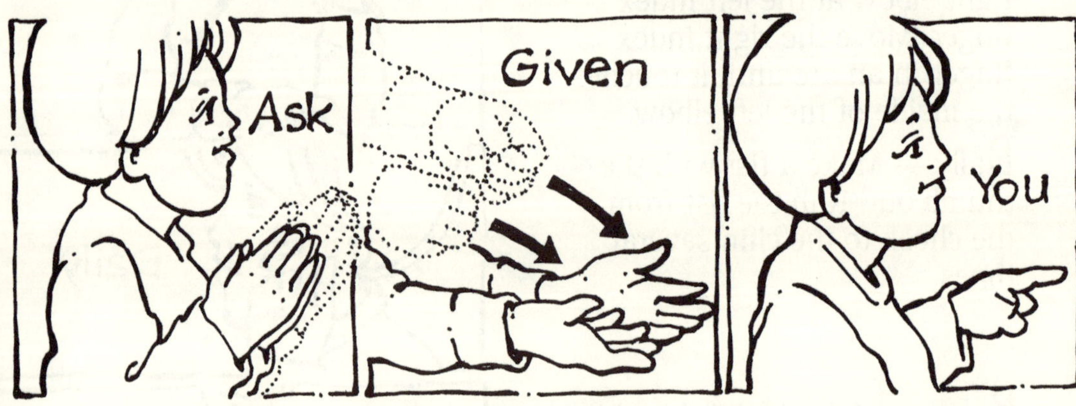

Ask — Hold hands palm to palm. Move palms toward body.

Given — Touch thumb and fingertips on each hand. Have hands facing palm down. Turn hands palms up. Flatten hands as you move them forward.

You — Point out with your index finger.

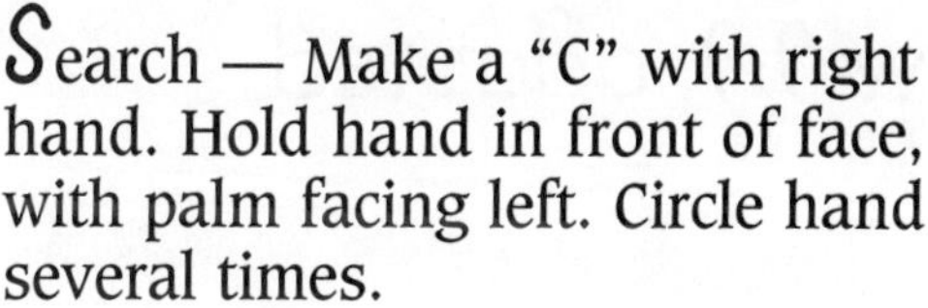

Search — Make a "C" with right hand. Hold hand in front of face, with palm facing left. Circle hand several times.

Find — Hold hand open, with palm down. Touch index finger to thumb and move hand up.

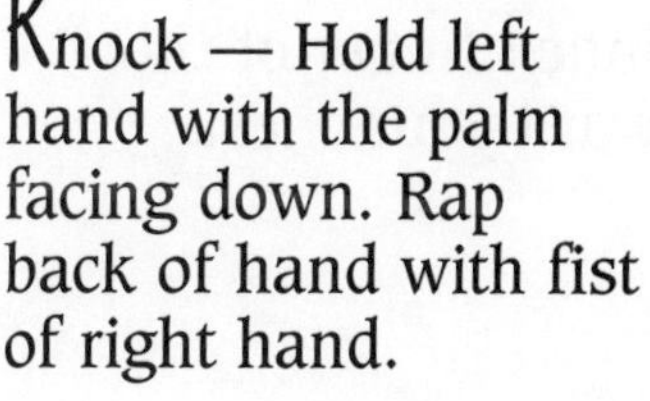

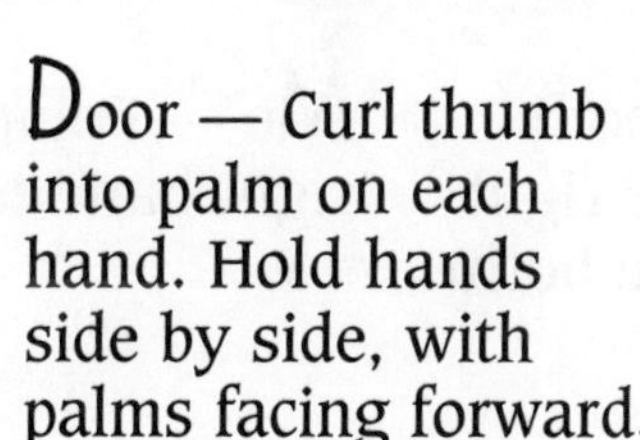

Knock — Hold left hand with the palm facing down. Rap back of hand with fist of right hand.

Door — Curl thumb into palm on each hand. Hold hands side by side, with palms facing forward.

Open — Hold hands side by side for the word *door*. Swing the right hand (thumb side) back and forth.

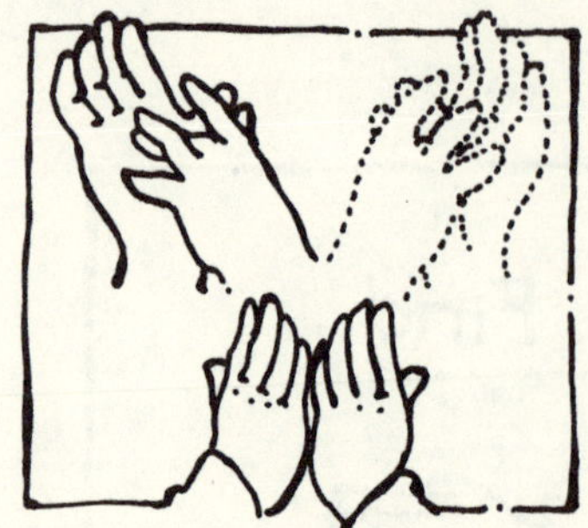

Jesus said, "Follow me."
Matthew 9:9, adapted

Follow — Make a fist with both hands, thumbs out. Hold the right fist behind the left fist. Move both fists forward.

Me — Point index finger of the right hand toward your chest.

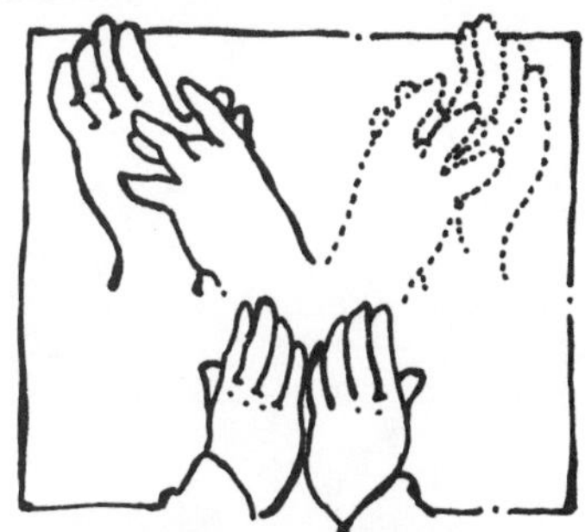

BIBLE VERSE:

Let the little children come to me.

Mark 10:14

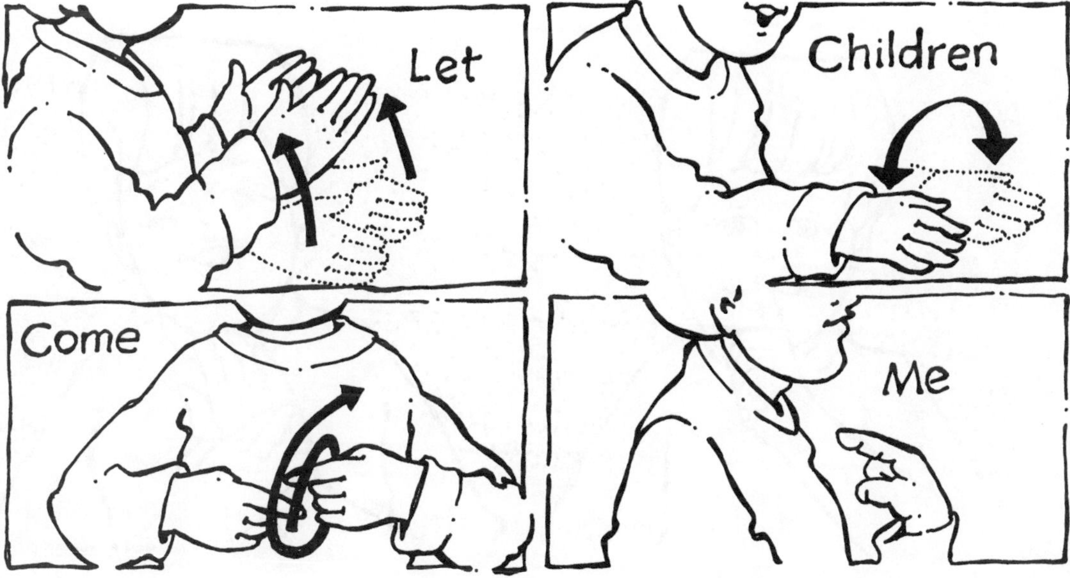

Let — Hold hands with palms facing each other. Move the fingers up and out until the heels of the hands are closer together than the fingers.

Children — Hold one hand palm down. Pretend to pat the head of a child. Repeat several times.

Come — Extend index fingers on both hands. Circle fingers around each other toward the body.

Me — Point index finger of the right hand toward your chest.

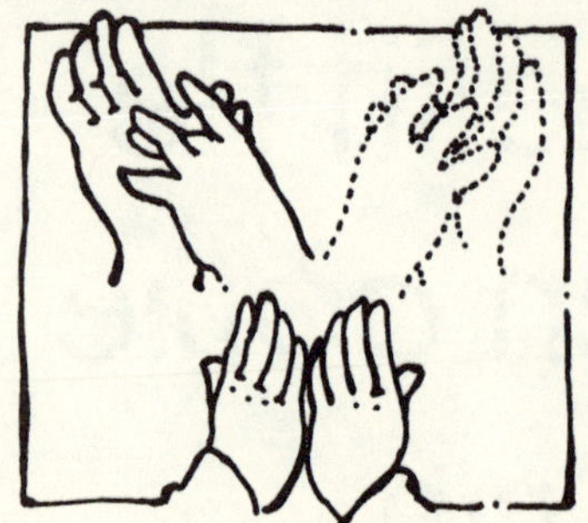

Hosanna!

Mark 11:9

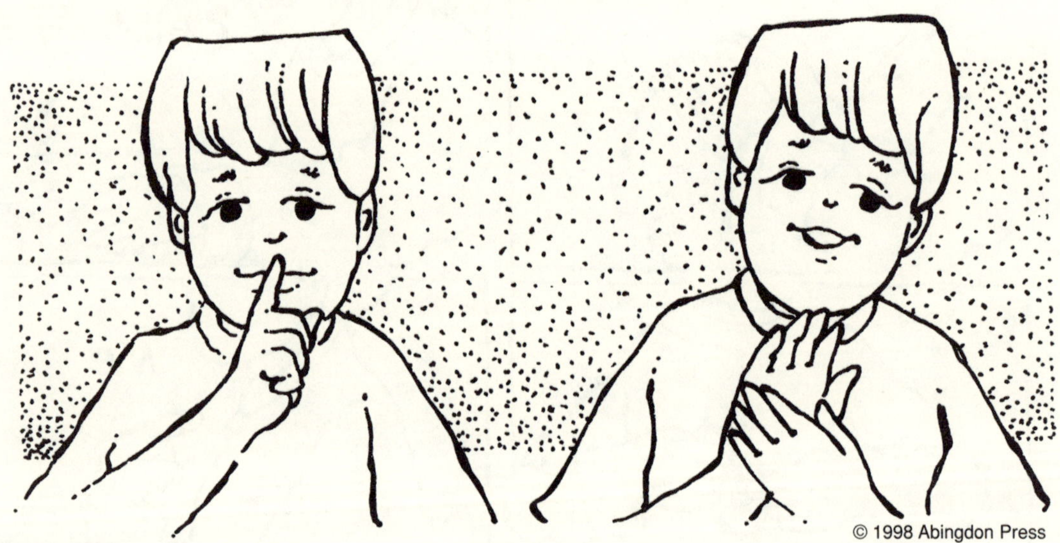

Hosanna — Touch the index finger of the right hand to the lips. Hold your left palm facing up. Make your right hand flat with palm facing down. Pat the right palm to the left palm.

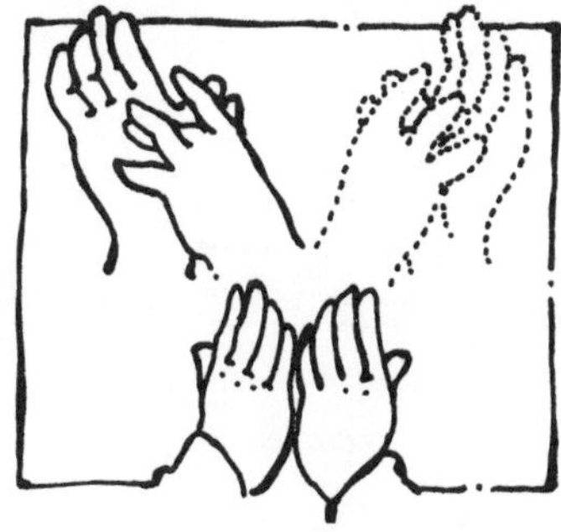

You will name him Jesus.

Luke 1:31

*Y*ou — Point out with your index finger.

*N*ame — Extend first two fingers of both hands. Place the fingers of the right hand across the fingers of the left hand, forming an X.

*J*esus — Touch the middle finger of the right hand to the palm of the left hand. Reverse.

29

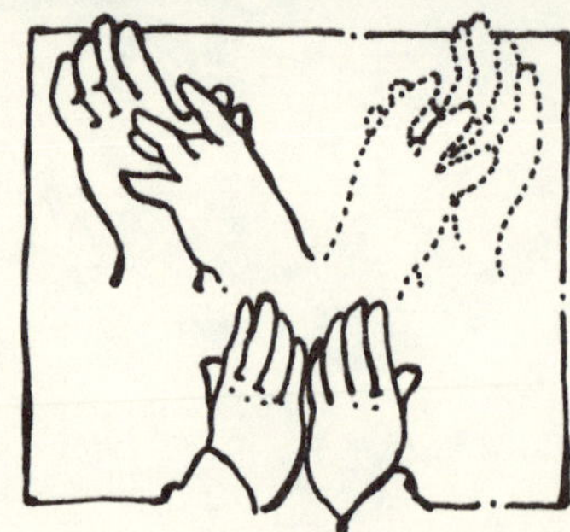

BIBLE VERSE:

I am bringing you good news of great joy for all the people.

Luke 2:10

I — Hold up little finger with the other fingers curled down. Place at chest.

Bringing — Hold both hands palms up, with one hand behind the other. Move hands away from body.

You — Point out with your index finger.

Good — Touch fingers of the right hand to the lips. Move hand down and place it palm up in the left hand.

News — Touch tips of fingers and thumbs on each hand and place at forehead. Move hands down and away, End with palms up.

Great — Raise both hands up, with palms facing forward.

Joy — Open both hands, with palms facing toward the chest. Pat the chest several times while moving the hands upward.

All — Hold the left palm toward the body. Circle the right hand out and around the left hand. End with the back of the right hand in the open left hand.

People — Touch middle finger to thumb on each hand. Circle hands towards the center with alternating motions.

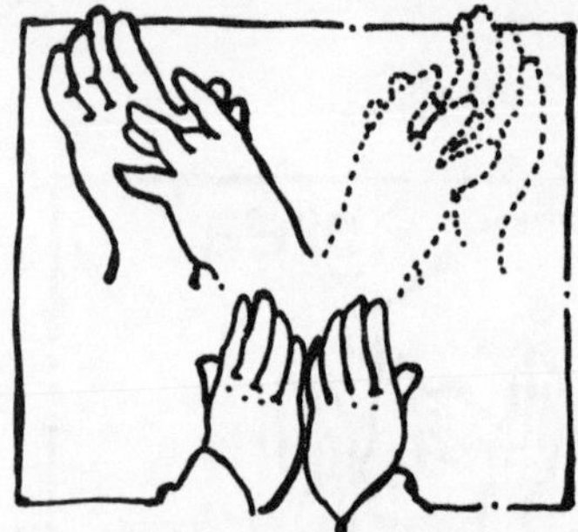

BIBLE VERSE:

Jesus grew both in body and in wisdom.

Luke 2:52, *Good News Bible*

Jesus — Touch the middle finger of the right hand to the palm of the left hand. Reverse.

Grew — Let the thumb and fingers of the left hand form an open circle, with the palm facing right. Push the right open hand up through the left hand.

Body — Touch your chest with both open palms. Repeat motion slightly lower on body.

Wisdom — Bend the index finger of the right hand. Move the bent finger up and down in front of the forehead.

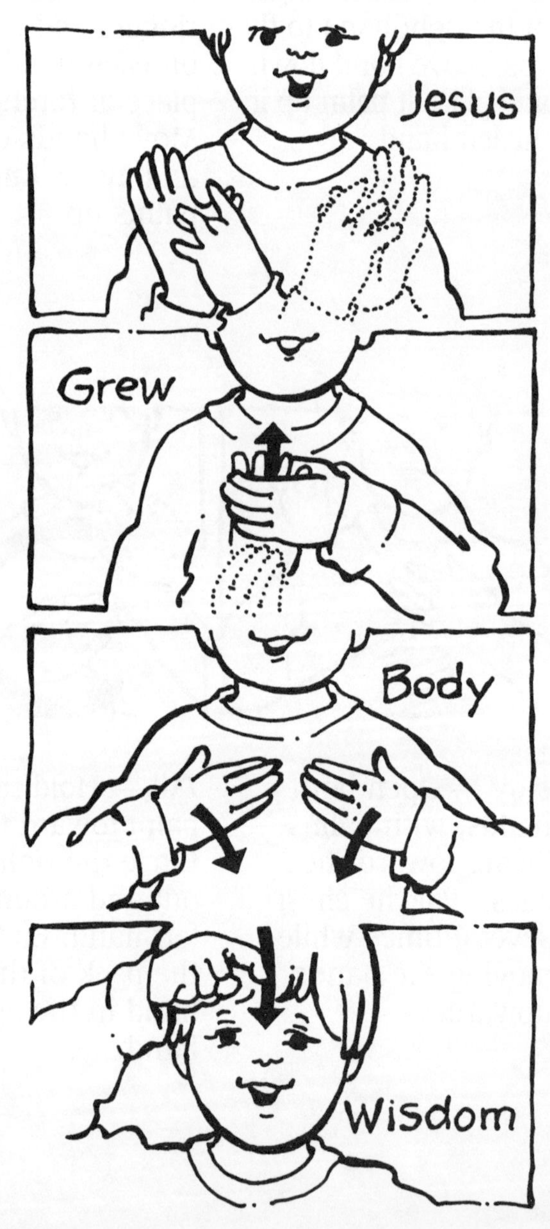

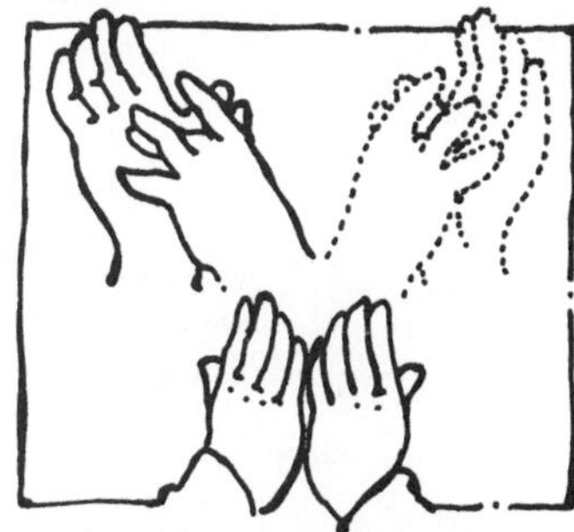

BIBLE VERSE:

Love your neighbor as yourself.

Luke 10:27, adapted

Love — Cross hands at wrist and press over heart.

Your — Hold up your hand, with the palm facing out.

Neighbor — Hold up both hands, with fingers slightly bent and palms facing the body. Move the right hand toward the inside of the left hand. Move hands to be parallel, with palms facing each other. Bring hands down.

Yourself — Hold hand in a fist, with the thumb out. Move fist quickly away from your body several times.

33

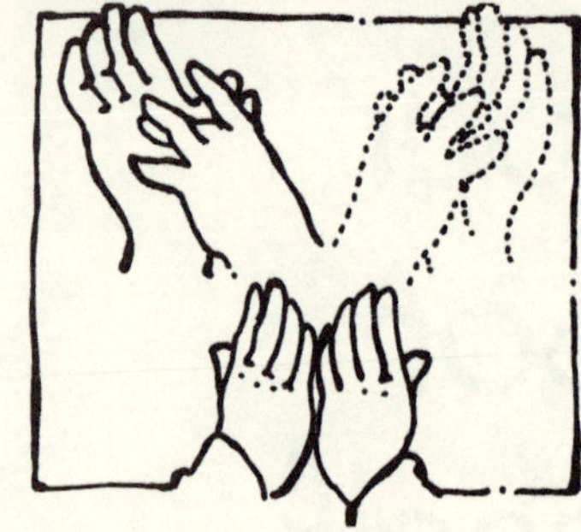

BIBLE VERSE:

For God so loved
the world that he gave
his only Son, so that
everyone who believes
in him may not perish
but may have eternal life.

John 3:16

34

God — Point the index finger of your right hand, with the other fingers curled down. Bring the hand down and open the palm.

Loved — Cross hands at wrist and press over heart.

World — Hold out three fingers on each hand (like a W). Circle the right hand around the left hand. Place the side of the right hand on the thumb of the left hand.

Gave — Touch thumb and fingertips together on each hand. Have hands facing palm down. Turn hands palms up and flatten hands as you move hands forward.

Only — Extend the index finger of the right hand. Hold the hand with the palm facing out and then twist the hand so that the palm faces the body.

Son — Bend fingers and thumb of the right hand as if grasping the bill of a hat. Place the hand at your forehead. Then bring the hand down to rest, palm up, inside the elbow of the bent left arm.

Everyone — Make fists with both hands, thumbs out. Hold up the left fist. Use the thumb of the right fist to stroke down the left thumb. Then hold up the index finger on right hand.

Believes — Touch your forehead with your right index finger. Bring hand down and flatten palm. Bring left palm up and clasp hands together.

Not — Make a fist with right hand, thumb out. Place thumb under chin and bring it forward.

Perish — Hold hands with right palm up and left palm down. Turn both hands over so that right palm is down and left palm is up.

Eternal — Point right index finger, palm up. Circle index finger in front of body. Change hand to hold out thumb and little finger, with palm facing down. Move hand forward.

Life — Extend the index finger and hold up the thumb to form an "L" with both hands. Move the "L" hands up in front of your body.

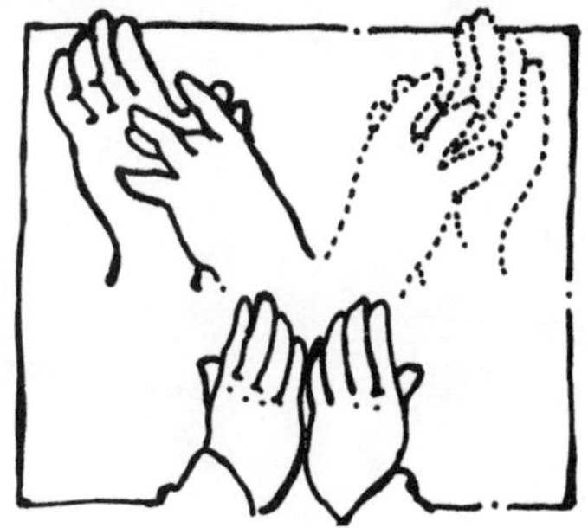

BIBLE VERSE:

Love one another.
John 15:17

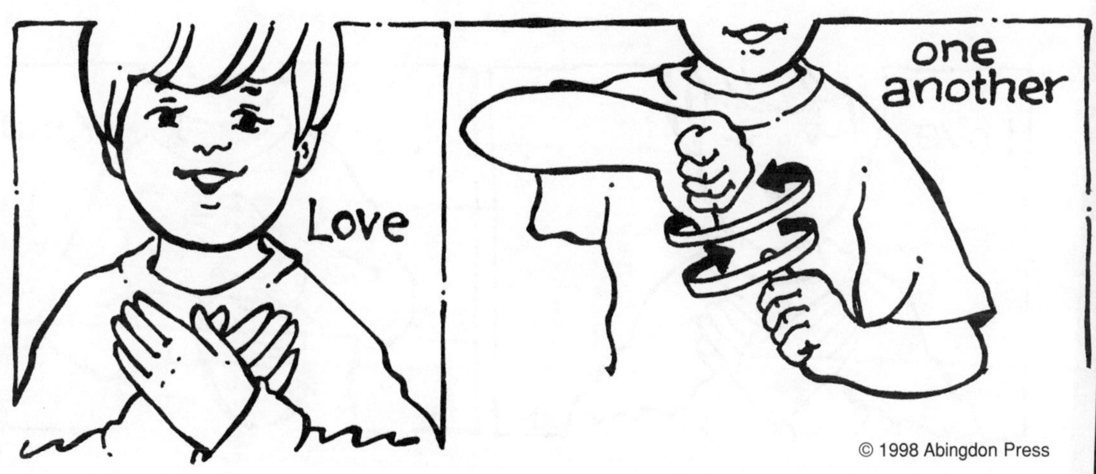

Love — Cross hands at wrist and press over heart.

One another — Make a fist with both hands, thumbs out. Hold right fist with the thumb down. Hold the left fist with the thumb up. Circle the thumbs counterclockwise around each other.

37

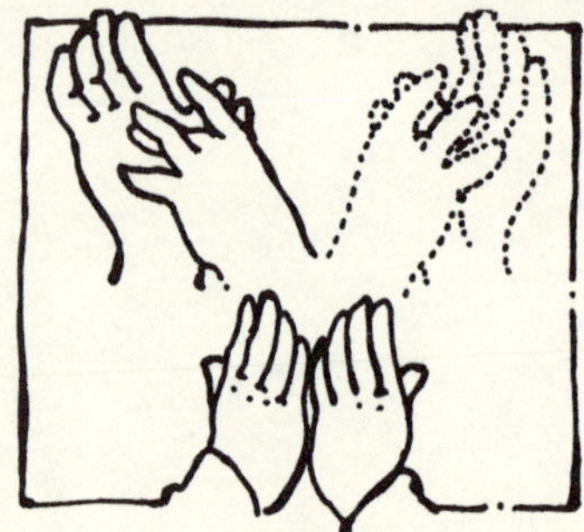

Love is kind.

1 Corinthians 13:4

Love — Cross hands at wrist and press over heart.

Kind — Place the right palm over the heart. Move the hand up and around the left palm.

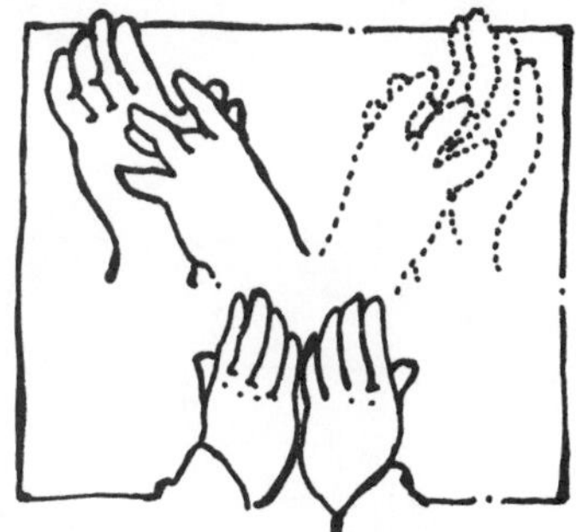

Love never ends.

1 Corinthians 13:8

Love — Cross hands at wrist and press over heart.

Never — Hold right hand with palm out near right side of your chest. Circle hand across in front of left shoulder and move hand abruptly off to the right side of the body.

Ends — Extend the little fingers of both hands. Move the right little finger down to strike the end of the left little finger.

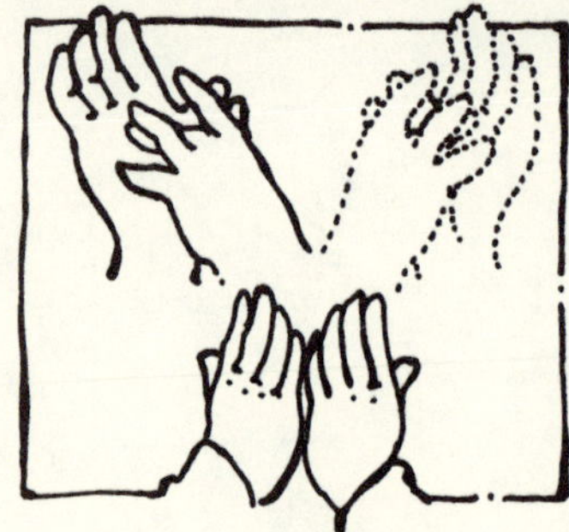

Now faith, hope, and love abide, these three; and the greatest of these is love.

1 Corinthians 13:13

Faith — Hold out right index finger. Touch your forehead with your right index finger. Then make fists with both hands, thumbs out. Hold up the fists to the left of the face, with the left fist above the right fist.

Hope — Touch your forehead with your right index finger. Move right hand out in front of forehead and open hand with palm down. Bend fingers. Move left hand with palm down to in front of forehead on the left and bend fingers.

Love — Cross hands at wrist and press over heart.

Abide (Stay) — Hold the right hand with the little finger and thumb extended. Move hand down in a short movement.

Three — Hold up the thumb and first two fingers of your hand.

Greatest — Raise both hands up, with palms facing forward.

Love — Cross hands at wrist and press over heart.

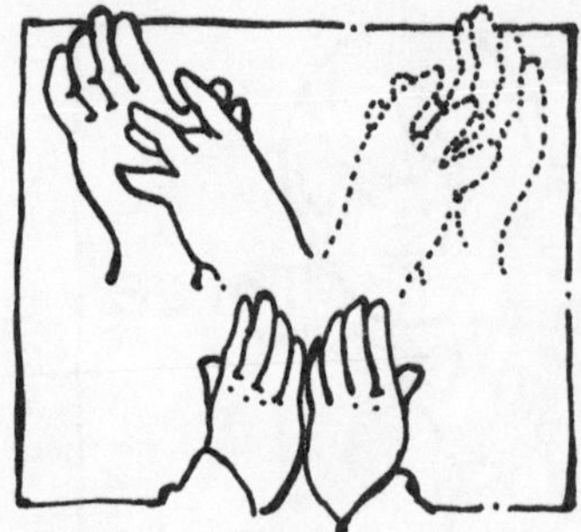

Be kind to one another.

Ephesians 4:32

Kind — Place the right palm over the heart. Then move the hand up and around the left palm.

One another — Make a fist with both hands, thumbs out. Hold right fist with the thumb down. Hold the left fist with the thumb up. Circle the thumbs counterclockbwise around each other.

42

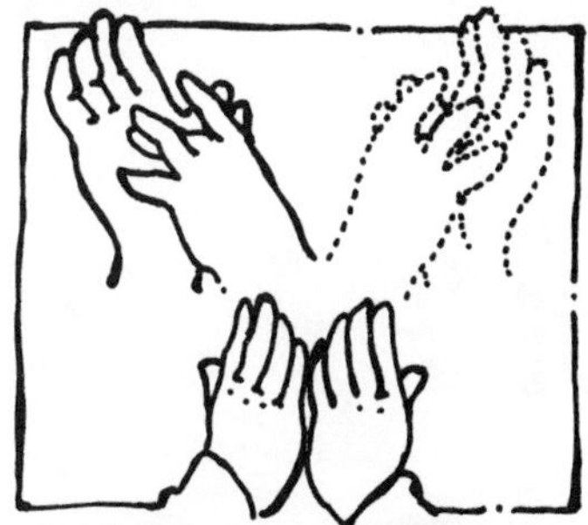

God cares for you.

1 Peter 5:7, adapted

God — Point the index finger of your right hand, with the other fingers curled down. Bring the hand down and open the palm.

Cares — Move open right hand past your face and toward left shoulder. Repeat motion with left hand.

You — Point out with your index finger.

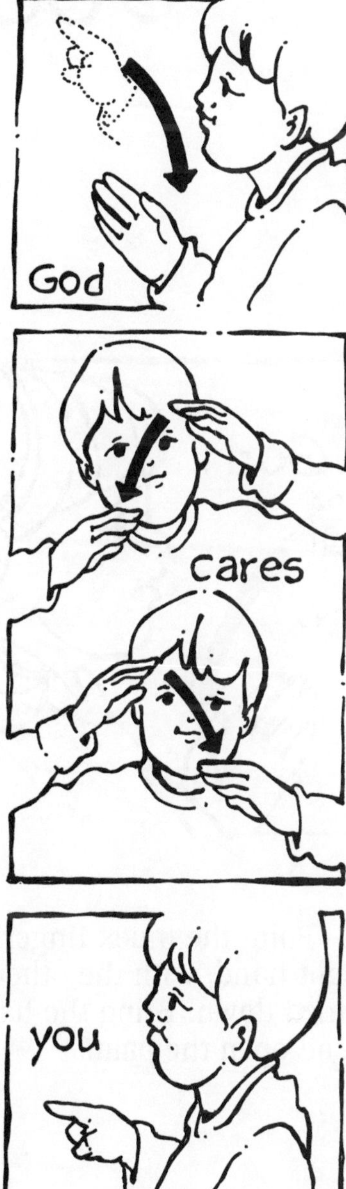

43

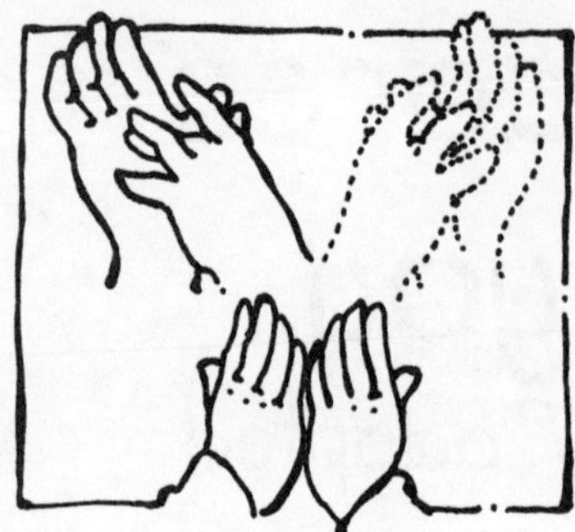

BIBLE VERSE:

God is love.
1 John 4:8

God — Point the index finger of your right hand, with the other fingers curled down. Bring the hand down and open the palm.

Love — Cross hands at wrist and press over heart.

Thank you, God

Thank you — Touch fingertips to lips and then move hands down and back, one at a time.

God — Point the index finger of your right hand, with the other fingers curled down. Bring the hand down and open the palm.

Jesus loves me

Jesus — Touch the middle finger of the right hand to the palm of the left hand. Reverse.

Loves — Cross hands at wrist and press over heart.

Me — Point index finger of the right hand toward your chest.

Alphabetical Index

Scripture Index

Old Testament

Exodus
God said, "I will be with you." (Exodus 3:12, adapted) — page 7

Deuteronomy
You shall love the LORD your God with all your heart, and with all your soul, and with all your might.
(Deuteronomy 6:5) — page 8

1 Samuel
The LORD looks on the heart.
(1 Samuel 16:7) — page 10

Psalms
The LORD is my shepherd.
(Psalm 23:1) — page 11
The LORD is my light and my salvation.
(Psalm 27:1) — page 12
Trust in the LORD. (Psalm 37:3) — page 13
Make a joyful noise to the LORD.
(Psalm 100:1) — page 14
Sing praise to the LORD.
(Psalm 105:2, adapted) — page 15
I was glad when they said to me, "Let us go to the house of the LORD!"
(Psalm 122:1) — page 16

Proverbs
A friend loves at all times.
(Proverbs 17:17) — page 18

Isaiah
For a child has been born for us.
(Isaiah 9:6) — page 19

New Testament

Matthew
Blessed are the peacemakers, for they will be called children of God.
(Matthew 5:9) — page 20
You are the light of the world.
(Matthew 5:14) — page 22
Give us this day our daily bread.
(Matthew 6:11) — page 23
Ask, and it will be given you; search, and you will find; knock, and the door will be opened for you.
(Matthew 7:7) — page 24
Jesus said, "Follow me." (Matthew 9:9, adapted) — page 26

Mark
Let the little children come to me.
(Mark 10:14) — page 27
Hosanna! (Mark 11:9) — page 28

Luke
You will name him Jesus.
(Luke 1:31) — page 29
I am bringing you good news of great joy for all the people. (Luke 2:10) — page 30
Jesus grew both in body and in wisdom.
(Luke 2:52, *Good News Bible*) — page 32
Love your neighbor as yourself.
(Luke 10:27, adapted) — page 33

John
For God so loved the world that he gave his only Son, so that everyone who believes in him may not perish but may have eternal life. (John 3:16) — page 34
Love one another. (John 15:17) — page 37

1 Corinthians
Love is kind. (1 Corinthians 13:4) — page 38
Love never ends.
(1 Corinthians 13:8) — page 39
Now faith, hope, and love abide, these three; and the greatest of these is love.
(1 Corinthians 13:13) — page 40

Ephesians
Be kind to one another.
(Ephesians 4:32) — page 42

1 Peter
God cares for you.
(1 Peter 5:7, adapted) — page 43

1 John
God is love. (1 John 4:8) — page 44

Good News Words
Thank you, God. — page 45
Jesus loves me. — page 46

MORE SIGN & SAY

Bible Verses for Children

ILLUSTRATED BY Robert S. Jones
EDITED BY Daphna Flegal

Abingdon Press

Nashville

More Sign and Say Bible Verses for Children

Sign, Say, and Remember

Children remember more easily what they learn when you involve both their bodies and their minds—and we want them to remember Bible verses! *More Sign and Say Bible Verses for Children* will help your children learn Bible verses using the hand motions of American Sign Language. Use the simple steps listed below to learn these verses yourself and then teach the verses to your children.

- Look at the illustrations.
- Read the written directions.
- Practice, practice, practice! (You need to be able to sign the verse for the children without looking at the page.)

Thank you to Bob Geldreich and Peggy Jennings for their help with signing.

4

Contents

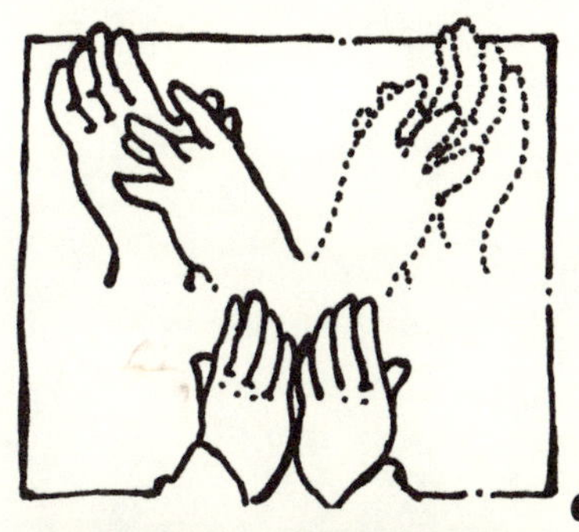

Then God commanded, "Let there be light."

Genesis 1:3, *Good News Bible*

God — Point the index finger of your right hand, with the other fingers curled down. Bring the hand down and open the palm.

Commanded — Point the first finger of your right hand to your mouth. Turn the finger out and then down. Make the motion strong.

Light — Bring both hands in front of your body, with the fingertips touching the thumbs. Move the hands up and apart in front of each shoulder. Open your hands and spread the fingers apart as you move.

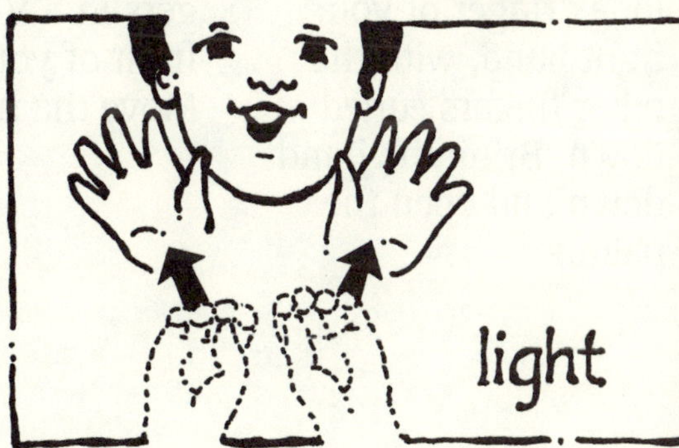

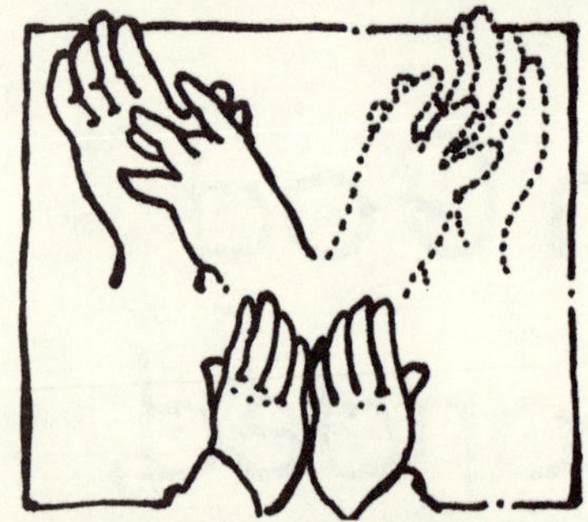

BIBLE VERSE:

And God saw that it was good.

Genesis 1:25

God — Point the index finger of your right hand, with the other fingers curled down. Bring the hand down and open the palm.

Saw — Hold your fingers in a V-shape in front of your eyes. Move the hand forward.

Good — Touch the fingers of your right hand to the lips. Move the hand forward and drop it into the open palm of the left hand.

BIBLE VERSE:

Respect your father and your mother.

Exodus 20:12, *Good News Bible*

Respect — Cross your first two fingers and touch your thumb to your last two fingers. This will make the letter "R." Bring the "R" in front of your face and down.

Father — Hold your right hand with the fingers spread apart. Touch the tip of the thumb to your forehead two times.

Mother — Hold your right hand with the fingers spread apart. Touch the tip of the thumb to your chin two times.

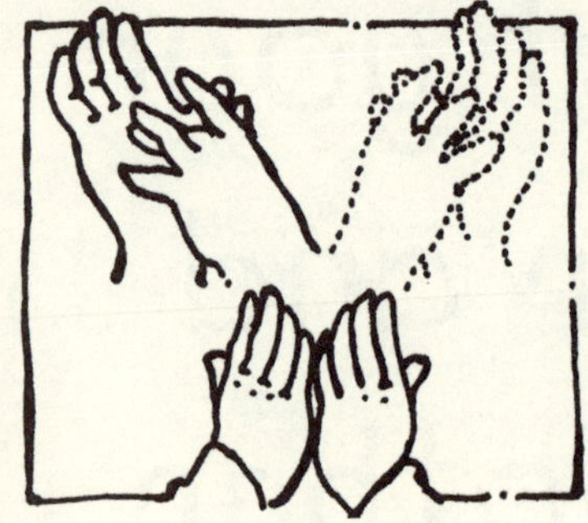

God is with you wherever you go.

Joshua 1:9

God — Point the index finger of your right hand, with the other fingers curled down. Bring the hand down and open the palm.

With — Hold both hands in fists, with the thumbs on the outside. Place the fists together, with the palms touching.

You — Point out with your index finger.

Wherever — Point your index finger and shake your hand back and forth. Then hold both hands with the palms facing up. Brush the fingertips of one hand with the fingertips of your other hand. Repeat the motion several times.

You — Point out with your index finger.

Go — Point your index fingers on both hands. Roll one hand forward over the other.

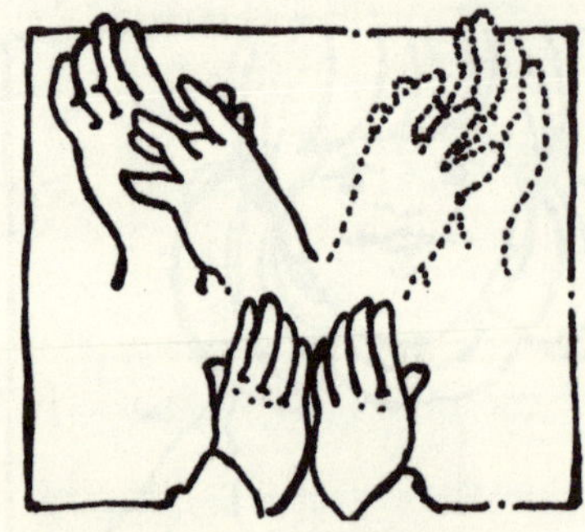

Serve the LORD with all your heart.

1 Samuel 12:20

Serve — Hold both hands palms up. Alternate moving your hands back and forth in front of your body.

LORD — Make an "L" with the right index finger and thumb. Place the "L" at the left shoulder and then move the "L" across the body to the right waist.

All — Hold the left palm toward the body. Circle the right hand out and around the left palm. End with the back of the right hand in the open left hand.

Heart — Draw an outline of a heart on the chest using the index fingers.

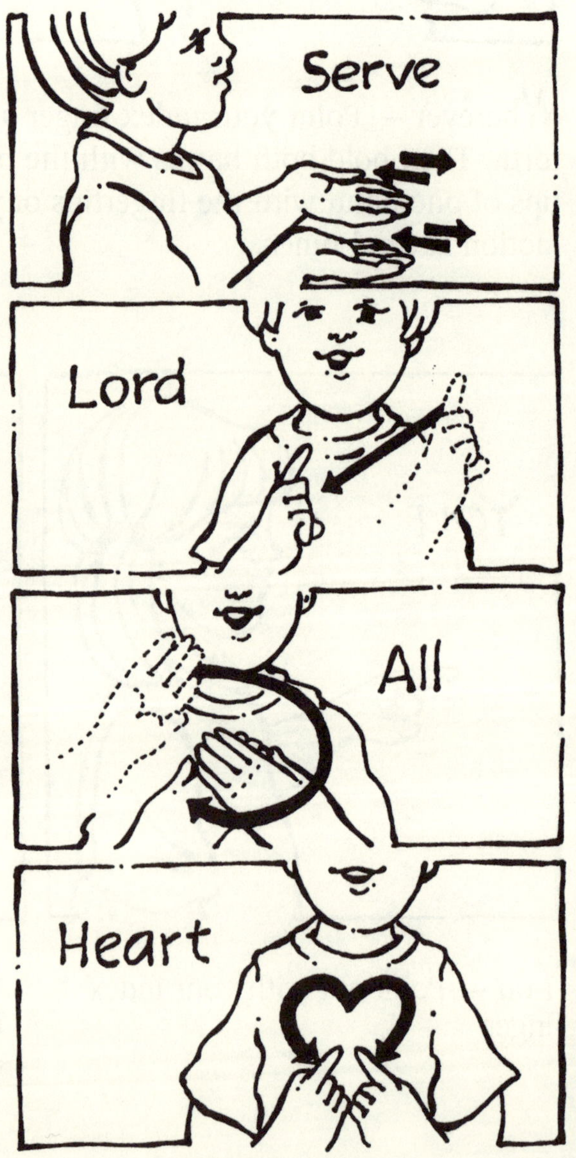

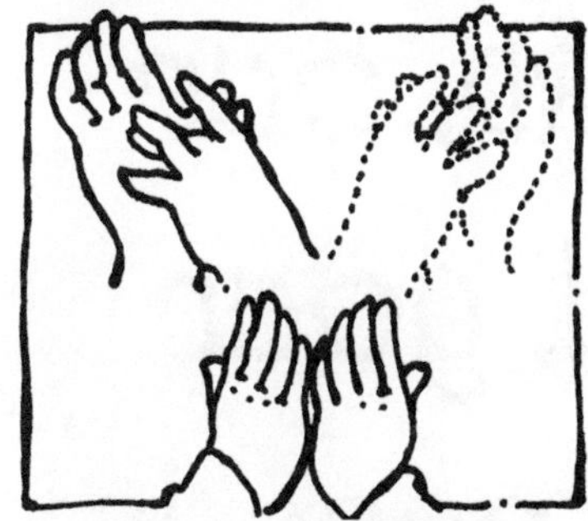

O give thanks to the LORD.

1 Chronicles 16:34

BIBLE VERSE:

Give — Touch your fingers and thumb together on each hand. The palms of the hands should face each other. Move the hands forward and open the fingers so that the palms face up.

Thanks — Touch the fingertips to the lips and then move the hands down and back, one at a time.

LORD — Make an "L" with the right index finger and thumb. Place the "L" at the left shoulder and then move the "L" across the body to the right waist.

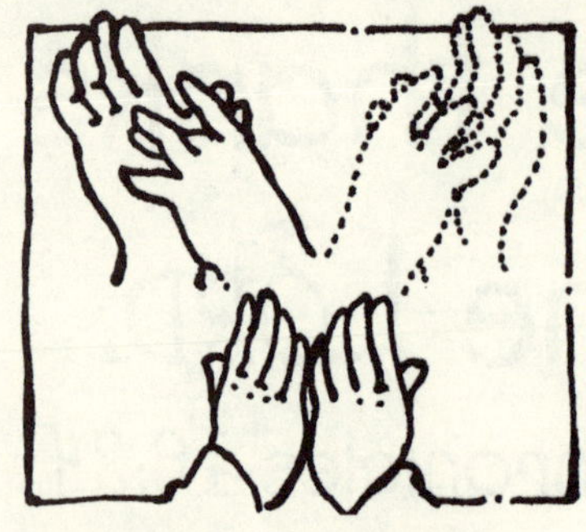

BIBLE VERSE:

O LORD, our Lord, your greatness is seen in all the world!

Psalm 8:1, *Good News Bible*

LORD — Make an "L" with the right index finger and thumb. Place the "L" at the left shoulder and then move the "L" across the body to the right waist.

Greatness — Raise both hands up with palms facing forward.

Seen — Hold your fingers in a V-shape in front of your eyes. Move the hand forward.

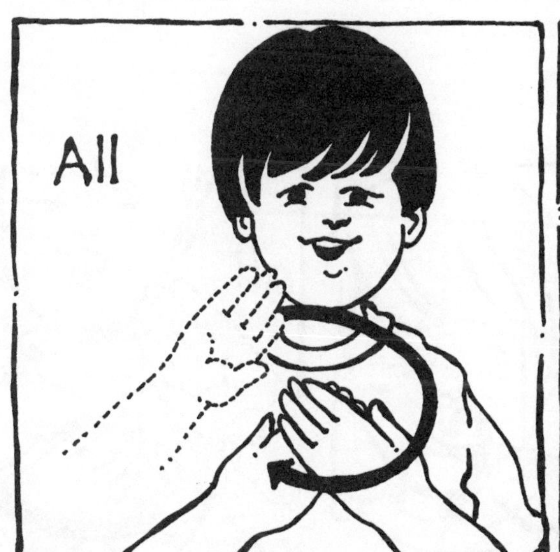

All — Hold the left palm toward the body. Circle the right hand out and around the left palm. End with the back of the right hand in the open left hand.

World — Hold out three fingers on each hand (like a sideways W). Circle the right hand around the left hand. End with the little-finger side of the right hand on the thumb of the left hand.

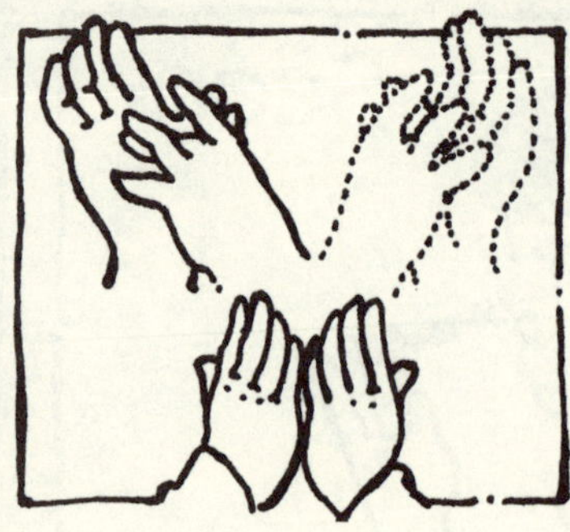

BIBLE VERSE:

I will tell of all the wonderful things God has done.

Psalm 9:1, *Good News Bible*, adapted

I — Hold up the little finger, with the other fingers curled down. Place the hand at the chest.

Tell — Hold your index finger at your chin. Move your finger forward and down.

All — Hold the left palm toward the body. Circle the right hand out and around the left palm. End with the back of the right hand in the open left hand.

Wonderful — Raise both hands up with the palms facing forward.

Things — Hold your hand in front of the body, with the palm up. Move your palm to the right and bounce it slightly.

God — Point the index finger of your right hand, with the other fingers curled down. Bring the hand down and open the palm.

Done — Form a "C" with each hand, with the palms facing down. Move your hands right and left several times.

17

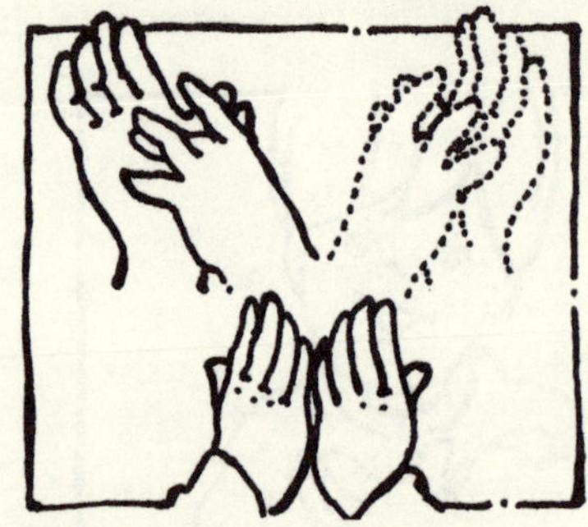

BIBLE VERSE:

The heavens are telling the glory of God.

Psalm 19:1

Heavens — Hold your palm toward your face, just over your head. Sweep your palm from left to right over your head.

Telling — Hold your index finger at your chin. Move your finger forward and down.

Glory — Clap your right hand on the open palm of your left hand. Then move your right hand up in an arc to the front of your right shoulder. Shake your hand as you move it.

God — Point the index finger of your right hand, with the other fingers curled down. Bring the hand down and open the palm.

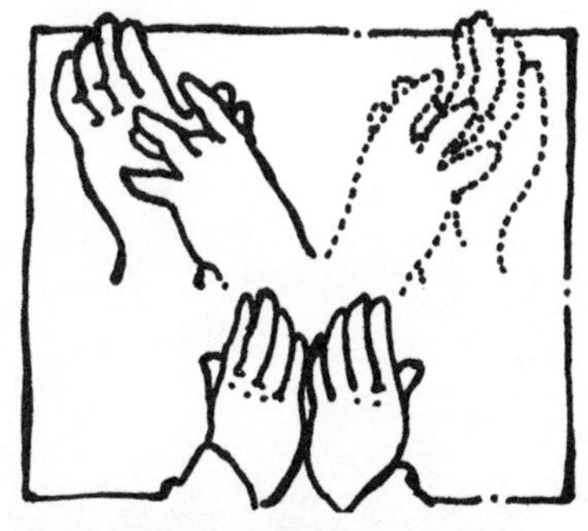

BIBLE VERSE:

O taste and see that the LORD is good.

Psalm 34:8

Taste — Touch the tip of your tongue with the middle finger of your right hand.

See — Hold your fingers in a V-shape in front of your eyes. Move the hand forward.

LORD — Make an "L" with the right index finger and thumb. Place the "L" at the left shoulder and then move the "L" across the body to the right waist.

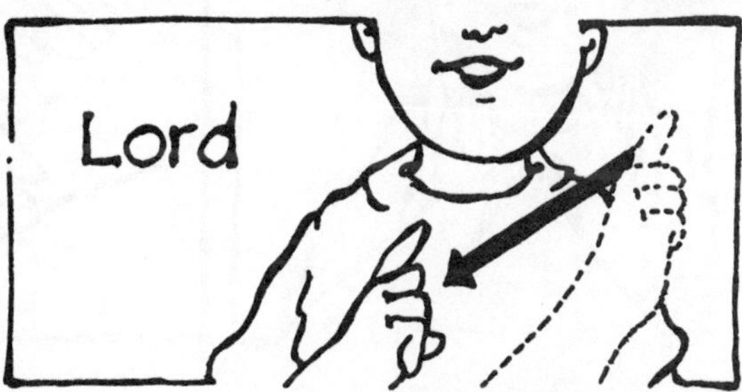

Good — Touch the fingers of your right hand to the lips. Move the hand forward and drop it into the open palm of the left hand.

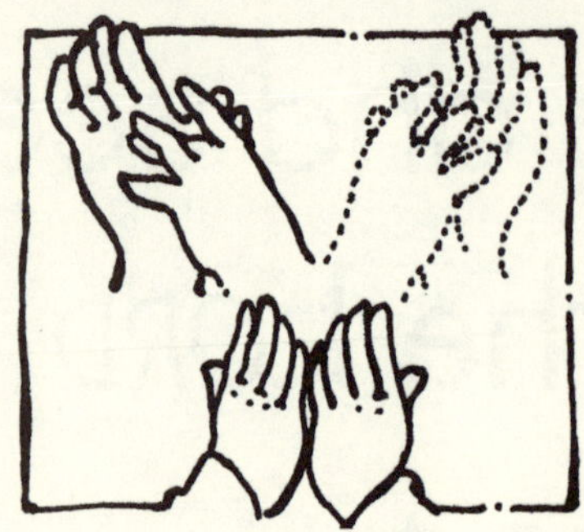

Clap your hands, all you peoples; shout to God with loud songs of joy.

Psalm 47:1

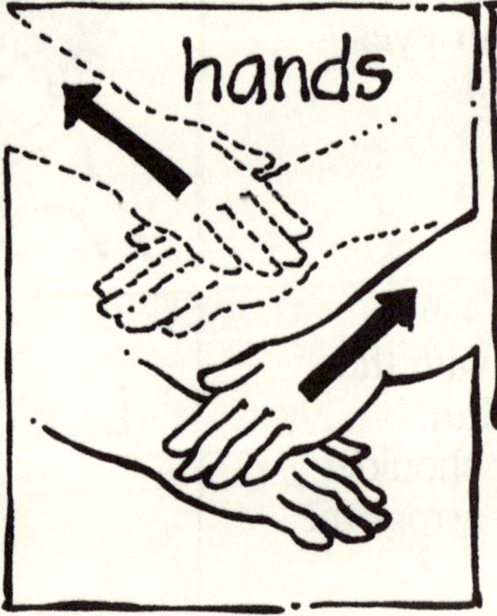

Clap — Clap your hands several times.

Hands — Use your right hand to stroke the back of your left hand. Then reverse.

All — Hold the left palm toward the body. Circle the right hand out and around the left palm. End with the back of the right hand in the open left hand.

Peoples — Touch the middle finger to the thumb on each hand. Circle your hands toward the center of your body with alternating motions.

Shout — Make a "C" shape with your right hand and place it in front of your mouth. Move your hand slightly up and to the side.

God — Point the index finger of your right hand, with the other fingers curled down. Bring the hand down and open the palm.

Loud — Touch your ear with your index finger. Then make fists with both hands and shake them back and forth in front of your body.

Songs — Hold out your left arm. Wave the fingertips of your right hand back and forth across your left arm.

Joy — Open both hands, with palms facing the chest. Pat the chest several times while moving the hands upward.

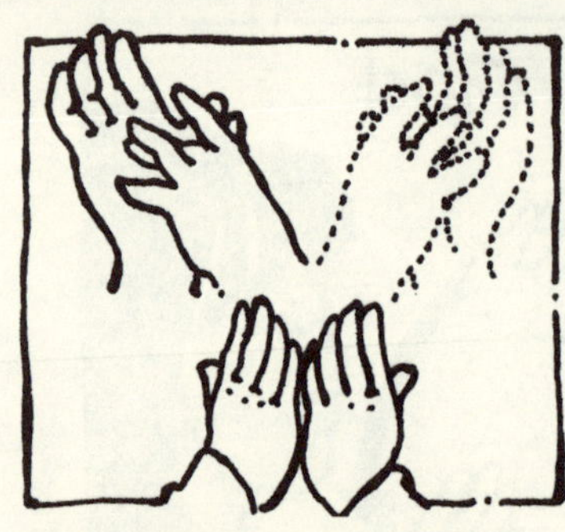

BIBLE VERSE:

God fills my life with good things.

Psalm 103:5,
Good News Bible, adapted

God — Point the index finger of your right hand, with the other fingers curled down. Bring the hand down and open the palm.

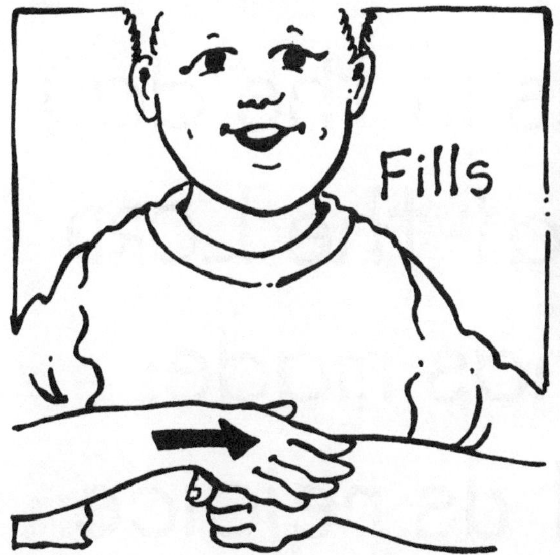

Fills — Hold your left hand in a fist with the thumb on the outside. Hold your right hand with the palm down. Brush your palm to the left over your fist.

Life — Hold each hand in an "L" shape. Move the "L" hands up the body from the waist to the chest.

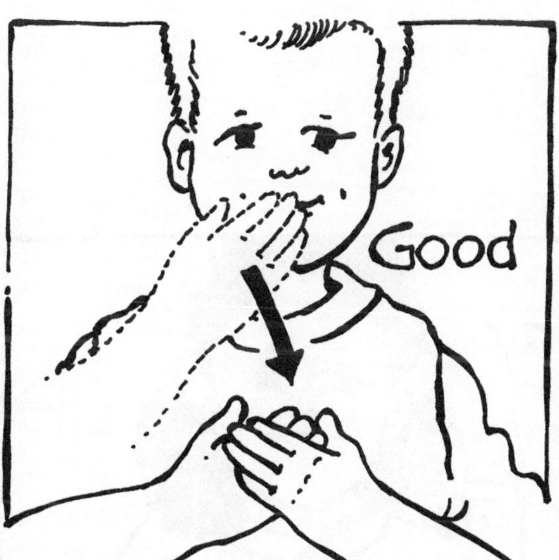

Good — Touch the fingers of the right hand to the lips. Move the hand down and place it palm up in the left hand.

Things — Hold your hand in front of your body, with the palm up. Move your palm to the right and bounce it slightly.

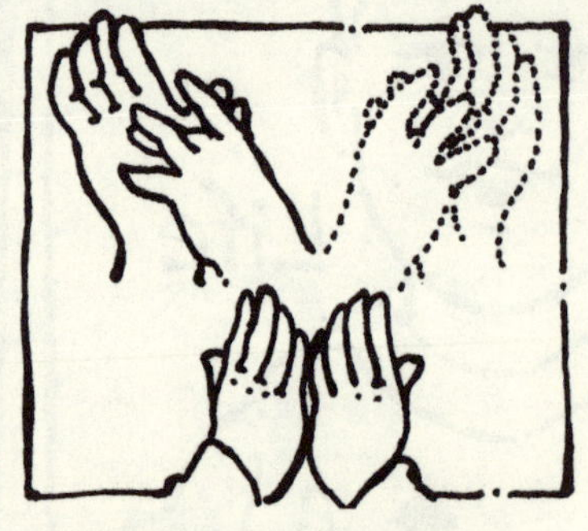

BIBLE VERSE:

This is the day that the LORD has made; let us rejoice and be glad in it.

Psalm 118:24

Day — Extend the index finger of the right hand. Hold the left arm parallel to the floor. Place the right elbow at the left index finger. Move the right index finger in an arc until it touches the inside of the left elbow.

24

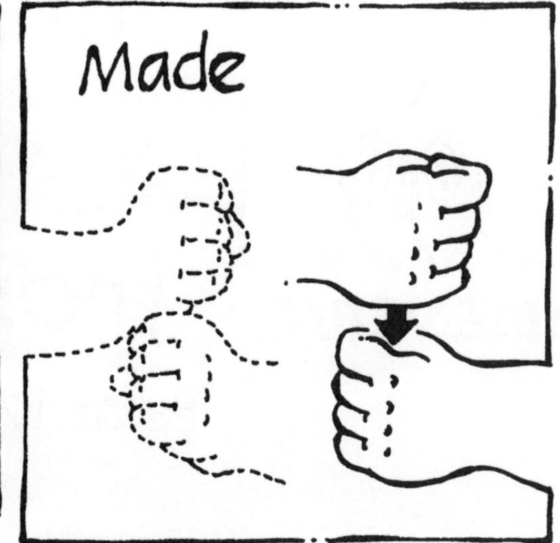

Lord — Make an "L" with the right index finger and thumb. Place the "L" at the left shoulder and then move the "L" across the body to the right waist.

Made — Make fists with both hands, with the thumbs out. Place the right fist on top of the left fist. Turn your fists so that the palms are facing your body. Pound the fists together again. Repeat the motion.

Rejoice and **G**lad — Open both hands, with the palms facing the chest. Pat the chest several times while moving the hands upward.

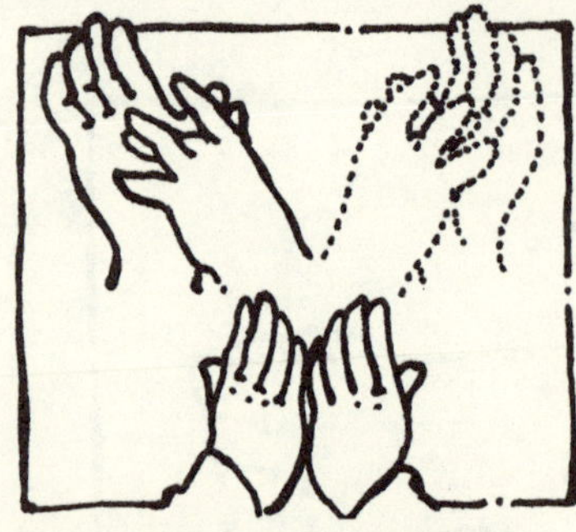

BIBLE VERSE:

Children are a gift from the LORD.

Psalm 127:3, *Good News Bible*

Children — Hold one hand palm down. Pretend to pat the head of a child. Repeat the motion several times.

Gift — Make fists with both hands, with the thumbs outside the fists. Hold the fists so that the palms face each other. Move the hands forward in an arc.

Lord — Make an "L" with the right index finger and thumb. Place the "L" at the left shoulder and then move the "L" across the body to the right waist.

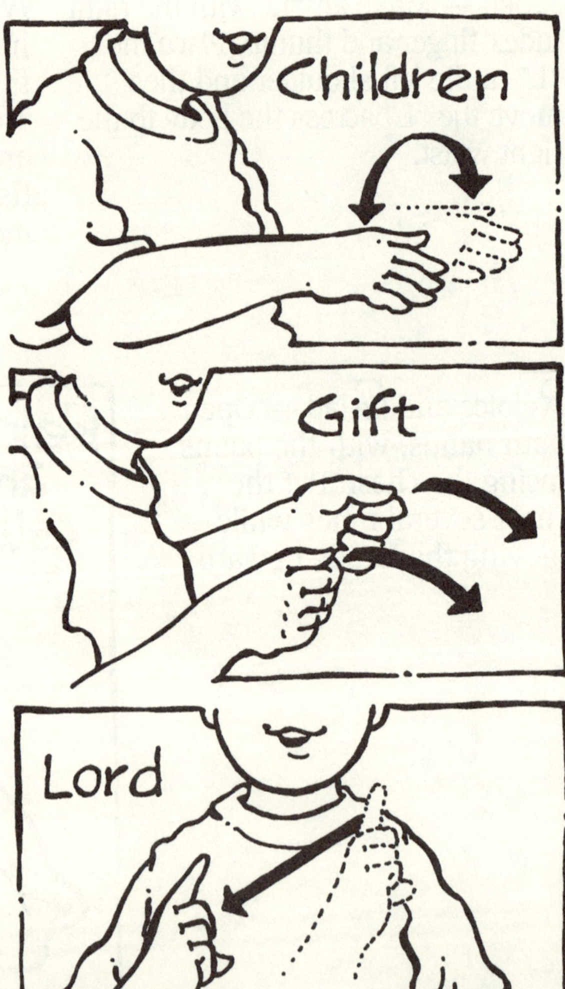

26

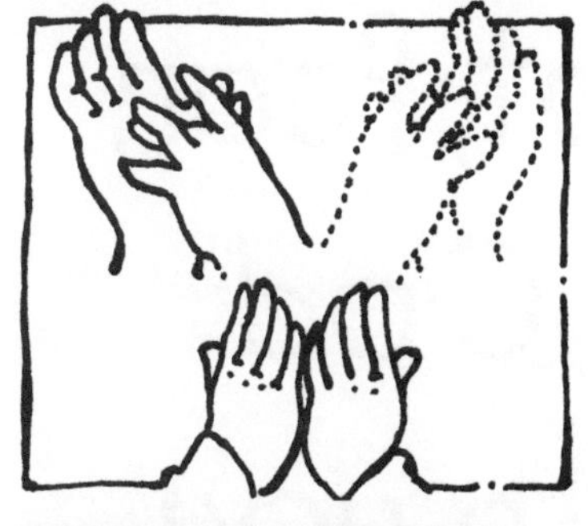

BIBLE VERSE:

Let everything that breathes praise the LORD!

Psalm 150:6

Everything — Make fists with both hands, with the thumbs out. Hold your fists so that the palms face each other. Use the thumb of the right hand to stroke down the thumb of the left hand. Then hold your hand in front of your body, with the palm up. Move your palm to the right and drop it slightly.

Breathes — Hold both hands open in front of the chest with the palms facing the chest. Move the hands in and out.

Praise — Clap your hands several times.

Lord — Make an "L" with the right index finger and thumb. Place the "L" at the left shoulder and then move the "L" across the body to the right waist.

27

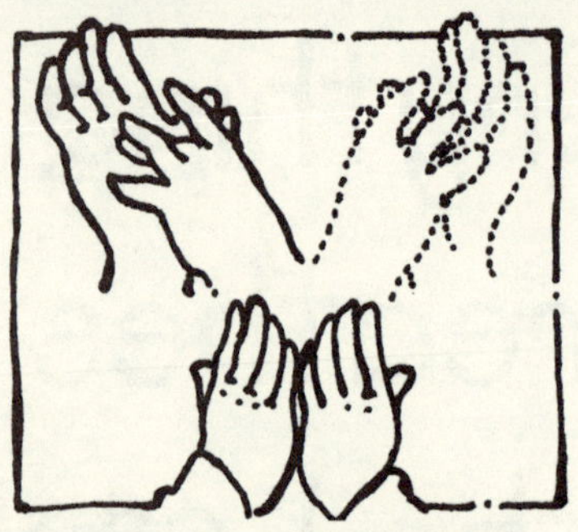

Do not fear, for God is with you.

Isaiah 41:10, adapted

Do not — Make a fist with the right hand, with the thumb out. Place the thumb of the fisted hand under the chin. Move the hand forward.

Fear — Hold both hands up with fingers spread, with the palms facing out. The right hand should be slightly behind the left hand. Bring both hands towards the body with a shaking motion.

God — Point the index finger of your right hand, with the other fingers curled down. Bring the hand down and open the palm.

With — Hold both hands in fists, with the thumbs on the outside. Place the fists together, with the palms touching.

You — Point out with your index finger.

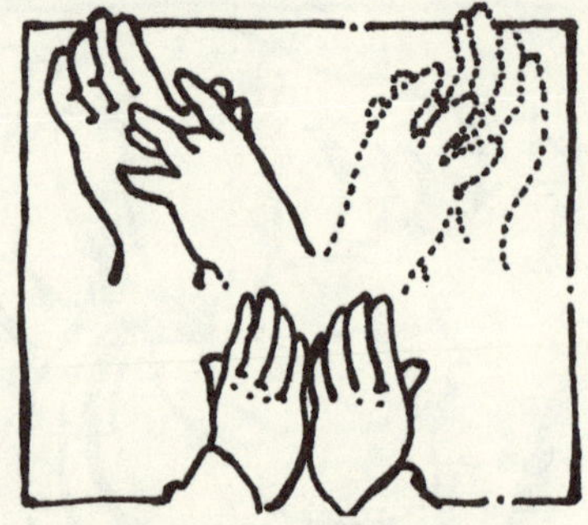

BIBLE VERSE:

And remember, I am with you always.

Matthew 28:20

Remember — Curl both hands into fists with the thumbs out. Touch the right thumb to your forehead. Bring your right fist down alongside of your face and then place your right thumb on top of your left thumb.

I — Hold up the little finger, with the other fingers curled down. Place the hand at the chest.

With — Hold both hands in fists, with the thumbs on the outside. Place the fists together, with the palms touching.

You — Point out with your index finger.

Always — Hold out your index finger with the palm facing up. Draw a circle in front of your body.

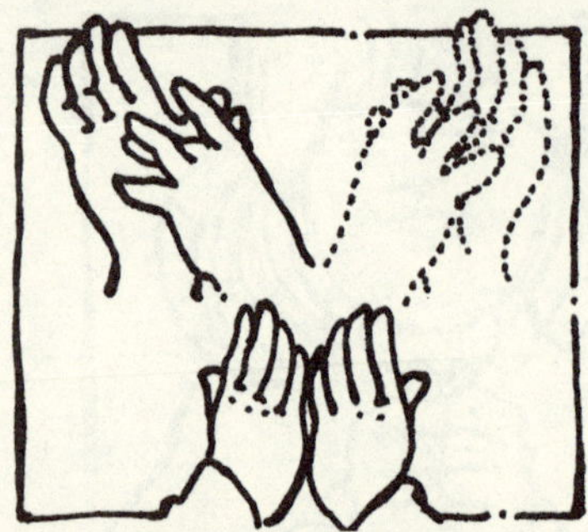

BIBLE VERSE:

Blessed is the one who comes in the name of the Lord!

Mark 11:9

Blessed — Make fists with both hands, with the thumbs out. Place both fists at the mouth. Bring the hands forward and down, opening the hands with the palms down.

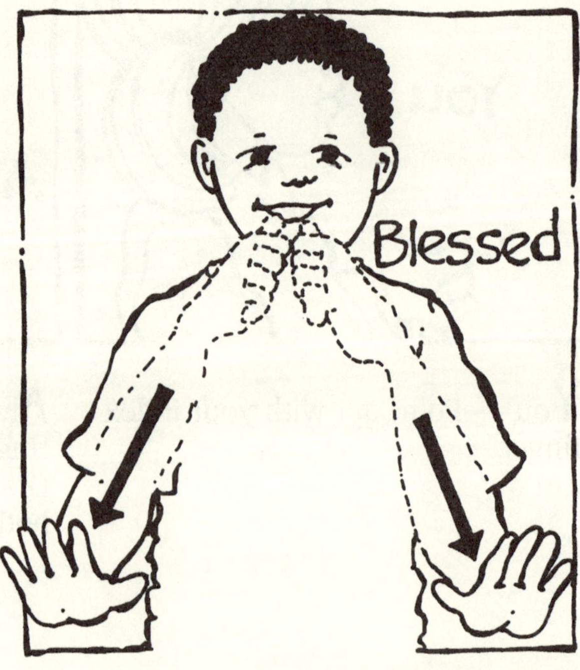

One — Hold up your index finger.

Comes — Extend the index fingers of both hands. Move the fingers toward the body as they rotate around each other once.

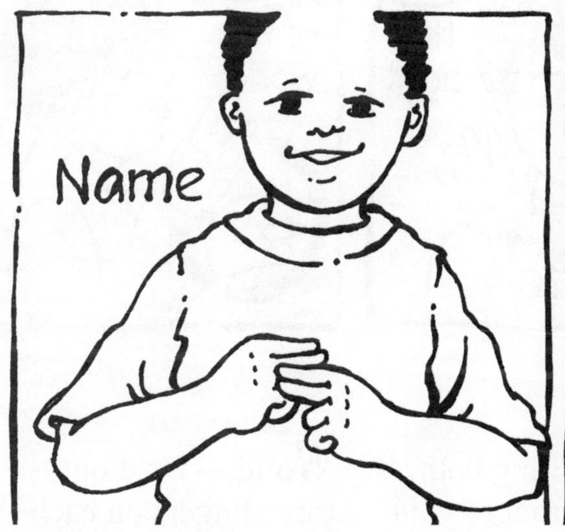

Name — Extend the first two fingers of both hands. Place the fingers of the right hand across the fingers of the left hand, forming an X.

Lord — Make an "L" with the right index finger and thumb. Place the "L" at the left shoulder and then move the "L" across the body to the right waist.

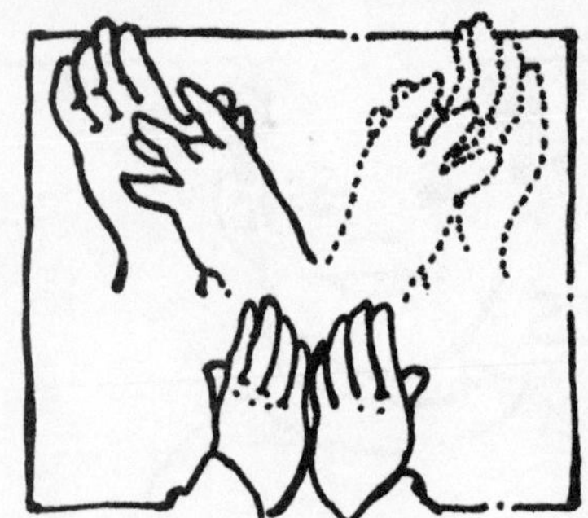

BIBLE VERSE:

I am the light of the world.

John 8:12

I — Hold up the little finger, with the other fingers curled down. Place the hand at the chest.

Light — Bring both hands in front of your body, with the finger-tips touching the thumbs. Move the hands up and apart in front of each shoulder. Open the hands and spread the fingers apart as you move.

World — Hold out three fingers on each hand (like a sideways W). Circle the right hand around the left hand. End with the little-finger side of the right hand on the thumb of the left hand.

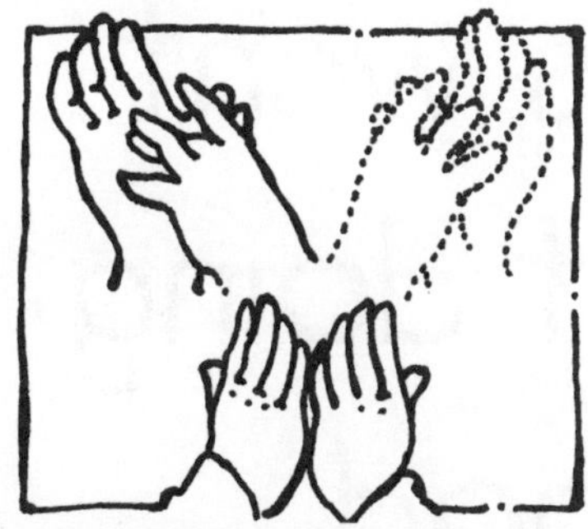

They all shared with one another.

Acts 4:32, *Good News Bible*

All — Hold the left palm toward the body. Circle the right hand out and around the left palm. End with the back of the right hand in the open left hand.

Shared — Hold out the left hand, with the palm up. Move the little finger side of the right hand back and forth across the left palm.

One another — Make fists with both hands, with the thumbs out. Hold the right fist with the thumb down. Hold the left fist with the thumb up. Circle the thumbs counter-clockwise around each other.

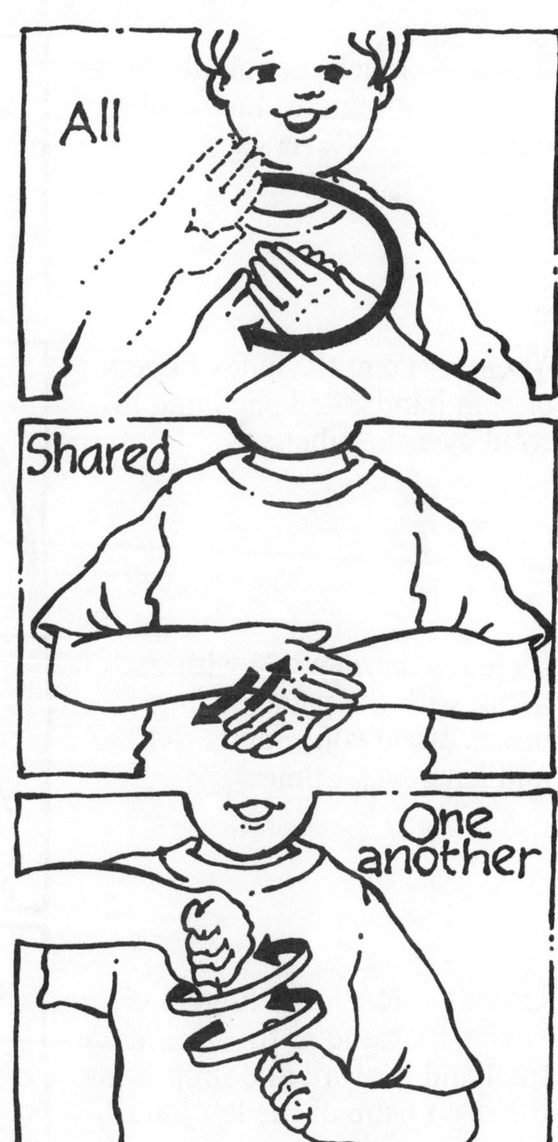

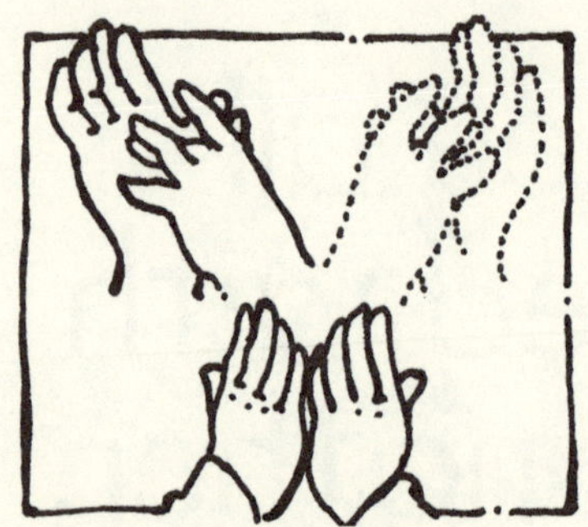

BIBLE VERSE:

Jesus went about doing good.

Acts 10:38, adapted

J esus — Touch the middle finger of the right hand to the palm of the left hand. Reverse.

W ent — Point the index fingers of both hands. Roll one hand forward over the other.

D oing — Form a "C" with each hand, with the palms facing down. Move your hands right and left several times.

G ood — Touch the fingers of your right hand to the lips. Move the hand forward and drop it into the open palm of the left hand.

BIBLE VERSE:

Love one another warmly as Christians.

Romans 12:10, Good News Bible

Love — Cross your hands at the wrists and press them over your heart.

One another — Make fists with both hands, with the thumbs out. Hold the right fist with the thumb down. Hold the left fist with the thumb up. Circle the thumbs counterclockwise around each other.

Christians — Make a "C" with the right hand. Place the "C" at your left shoulder and move it across your body to the right waist.

Hold both hands in front of your body with the palms facing each other. Bring both hands straight down.

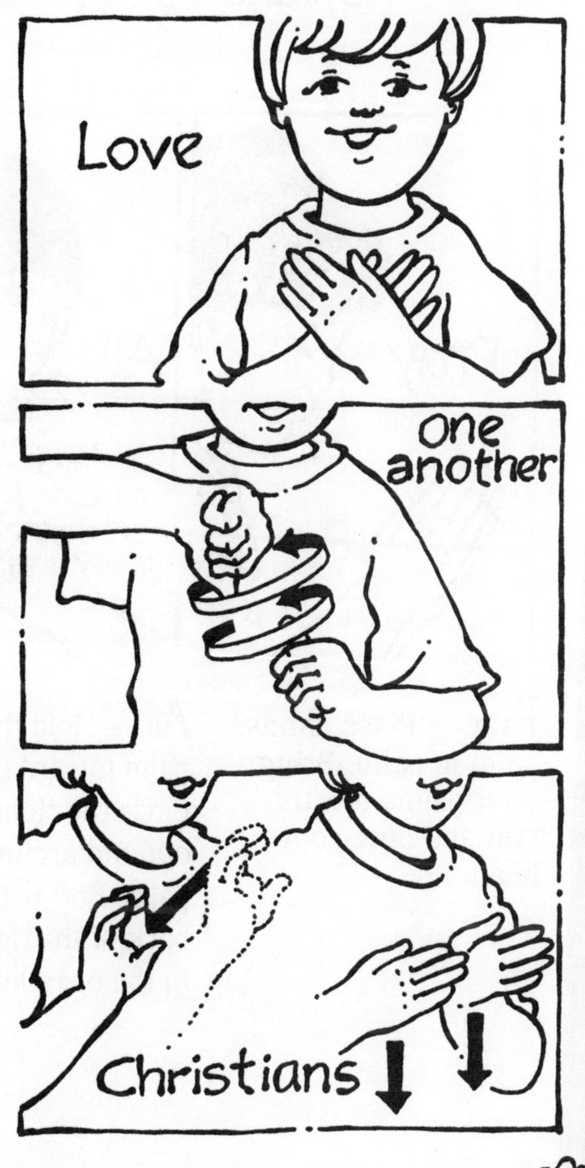

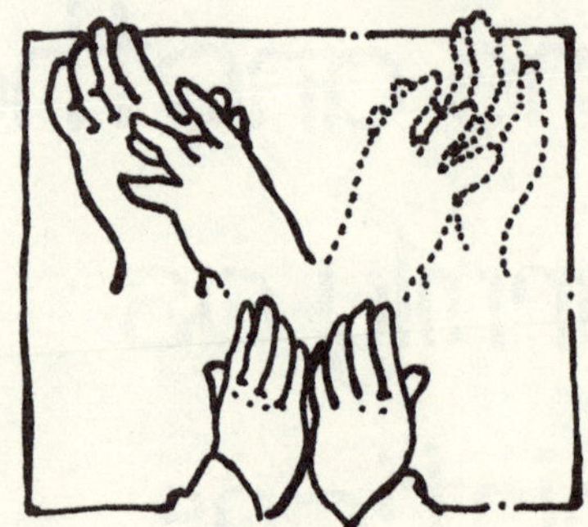

Pray at all times.

Romans 12:12, *Good News Bible*

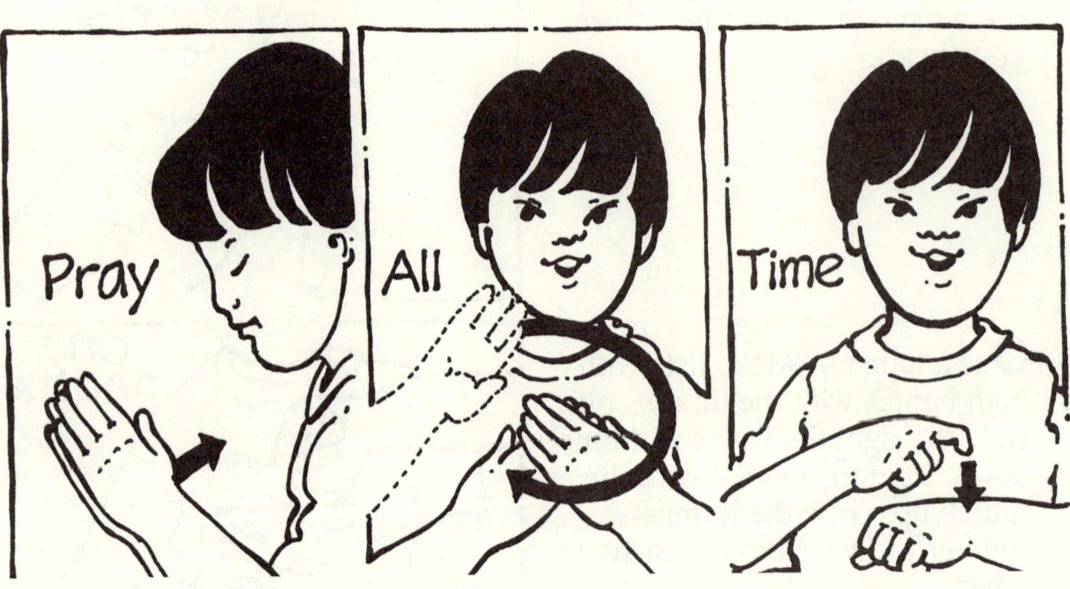

Pray — Place hands palm to palm. Bring your palms toward you and bow your head.

All — Hold the left palm toward the body. Circle the right hand out and around the left palm. End with the back of the right hand in the open left hand.

Times — Use the index finger of your right hand to tap the back of the left hand.

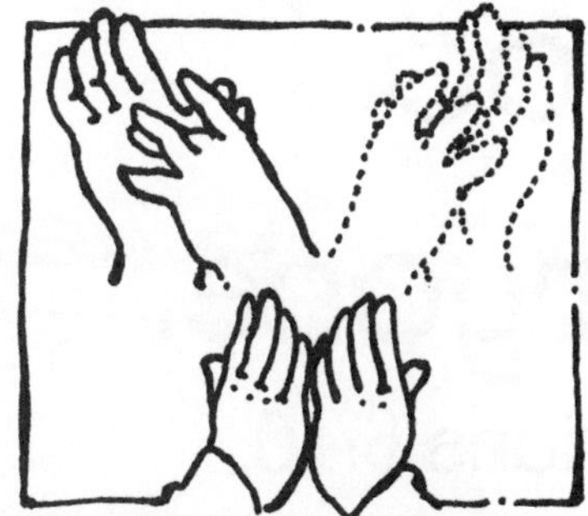

God loves a cheerful giver.

2 Corinthians 9:7

BIBLE VERSE:

God — Point the index finger of your right hand, with the other fingers curled down. Bring the hand down and open the palm.

Loves — Cross your hands at the wrists and press them over your heart.

Cheerful — Hold your hands with the fingers spread apart near the sides of your mouth. Wiggle your fingers as you move your hands up toward your ears.

Giver — Touch your fingers and thumb together on each hand. The palms of the hands should face each other. Move the hands forward and open the fingers so that the palms face up.

Hold both hands in front of your body with the palms facing each other. Bring both hands straight down.

39

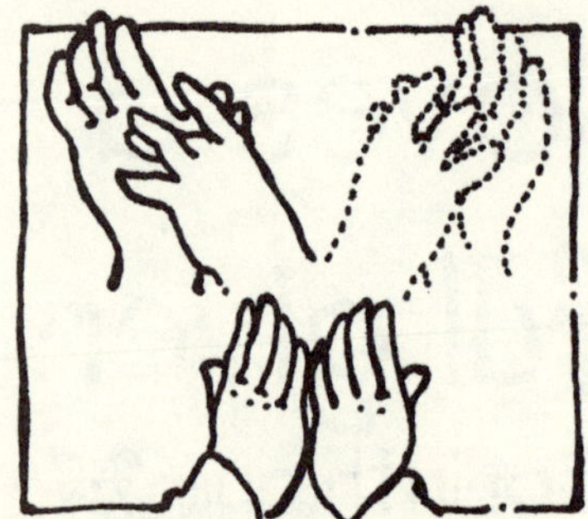

BIBLE VERSE:

Do good to everyone.

Galatians 6:10,
Good News Bible

Do —Form a "C" with each hand, with the palms facing down. Move your hands right and left several times.

Good — Touch the fingers of your right hand to the lips. Move the hand forward and drop it into the open palm of the left hand.

To — Hold up the index finger of your left hand. Move the index finger of your right hand to touch the index finger of your left hand.

Everyone — Make fists with both hands,with the thumbs out. Hold your fists so that the palms face each other. Use the thumb of the right hand to stroke down the thumb of the left hand.

Then hold up your index finger.

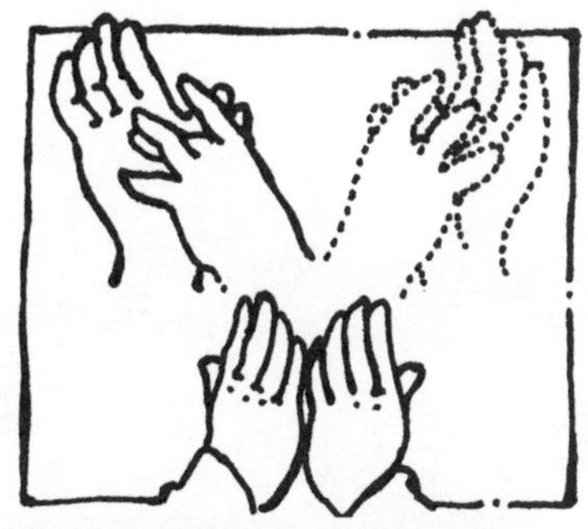

Children, obey your parents.

BIBLE VERSE:

Children — Hold one hand palm down. Pretend to pat the head of a child. Repeat the action several times.

Obey — Hold both hands in fists at eye level with the palms facing your body. Drop both hands down and open the fists with the palms facing up.

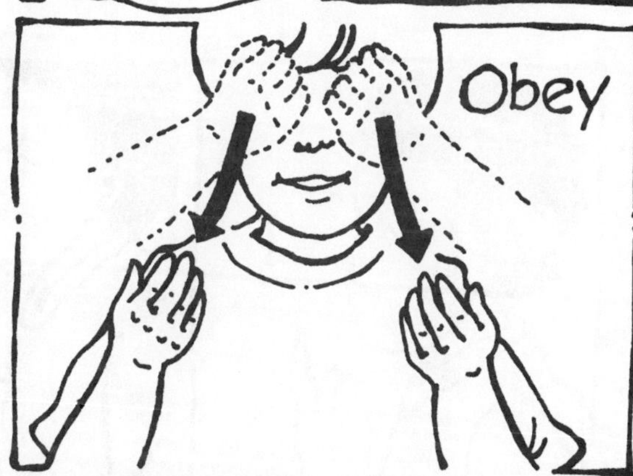

Parents — Make the signs for *father* and *mother*. **Father:** hold your right hand with the fingers spread apart. Touch the tip of the thumb to your forehead two times. **Mother:** hold your right hand with the fingers spread apart. Touch the tip of the thumb to your chin two times.

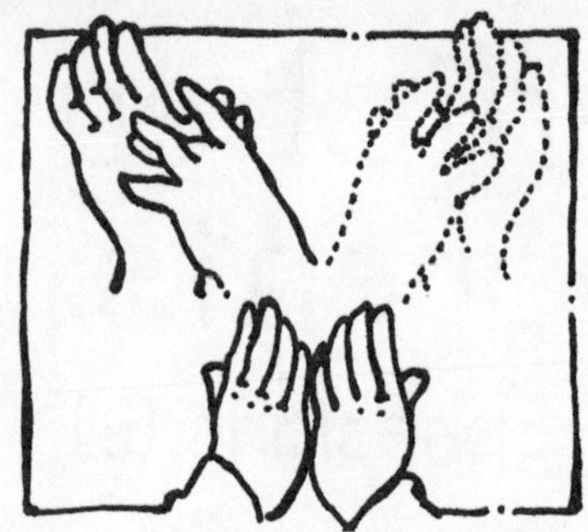

I can do all things through Christ who strengthens me.

Philippians 4:13, adapted

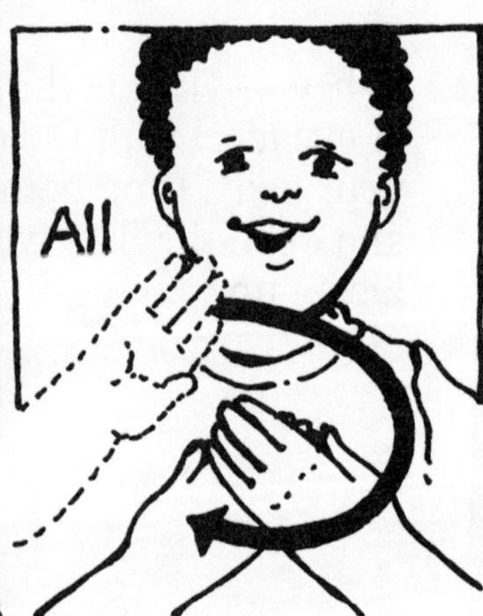

I — Hold up the little finger, with the other fingers curled down. Place the hand at the chest.

Do — Form a "C" with each hand, with the palms facing down. Move your hands right and left several times.

All — Hold the left palm toward the body. Circle the right hand out and around the left palm. End with the back of the right hand in the open left hand.

Things — Hold your hand in front of the body, with the palm up. Move your palm to the right and bounce it slightly.

Christ — Make a "C" with the right hand. Place the "C" at your left shoulder and move it across your body to the right waist.

Strengthens — Touch your fingers to the front of your shoulders. Then bring both hands forward and form fists.

Me — Point the index finger of your right hand toward your chest.

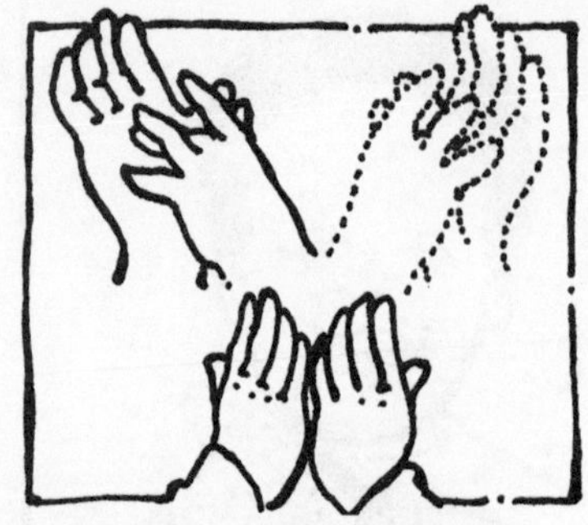

BIBLE VERSE:

For everything created by God is good.

1 Timothy 4:4

Everything — Make fists with both hands, with the thumbs out. Hold your fists so that the palms face each other. Use the thumb of the right hand to stroke down the thumb of the left hand. Then hold your hand in front of the body, with the palm up. Move your palm to the right and drop it slightly.

Created (made) — Make fists with both hands, with the thumbs out. Place the right fist on top of the left fist. Turn your fists so that the palms are facing your body. Pound the fists together again. Repeat the motion.

God — Point the index finger of your right hand, with the other fingers curled down. Bring the hand down and open the palm.

Good — Touch the fingers of your right hand to the lips. Move the hand forward and drop it into the open palm of the left hand.

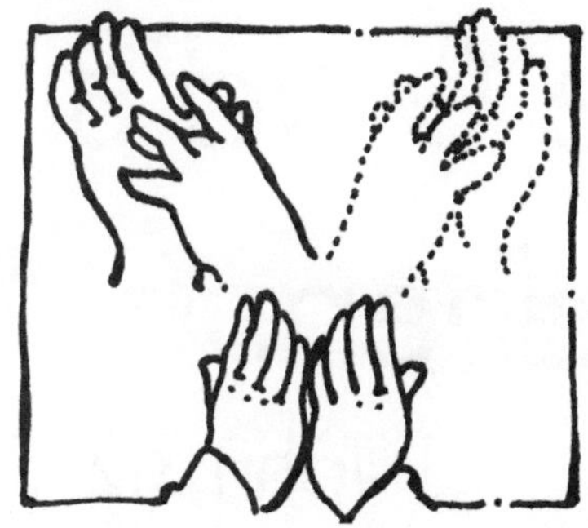

BIBLE VERSE:

Share what you have.

Hebrews 13:16

Share — Hold out the left hand, with the palm up. Move the little finger side of the right hand back and forth across the left palm.

You — Point out with your index finger.

Have — Hold both hands with the fingers bent. Touch the fingertips to your chest.

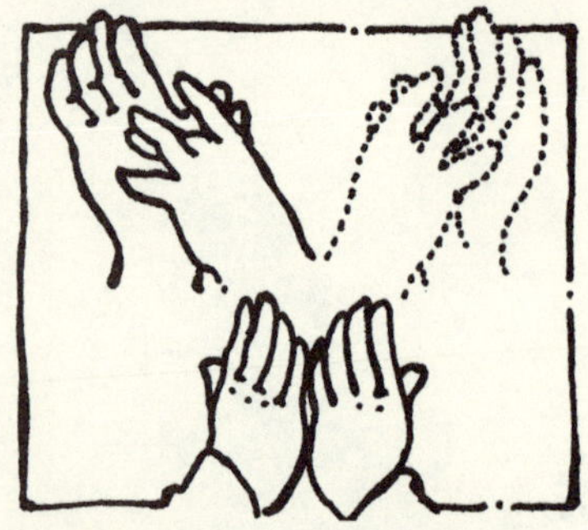

We are God's children.

1 John 3:2

We — Touch your right index finger to your right shoulder. Circle the finger out and then touch it to your left shoulder.

God — Point the index finger of your right hand, with the other fingers curled down. Bring the hand down and open the palm.

Children — Hold one hand palm down. Pretend to pat the head of a child. Repeat the motion several times.

Alphabetical Index

Scripture Index

Old Testament

Genesis
Then God commanded, "Let there be light."
(Genesis 1:3, *Good News Bible*) — page 7
And God saw that it was good.
(Genesis 1:25) — page 8

Exodus
Respect your father and your mother.
(Exodus 20:12, *Good News Bible*) — page 9

Joshua
God is with you wherever you go.
(Joshua 1:9) — page 10

1 Samuel
Serve the LORD with all your heart.
(1 Samuel 12:20) — page 12

1 Chronicles
O give thanks to the LORD.
(1 Chronicles 16:34) — page 13

Psalms
O LORD, our Lord, your greatness is seen
in all the world! (Psalm 8:1, *Good News
Bible*) — page 14
I will tell of all the wonderful things God
has done. (Psalm 9:1, *Good News Bible*,
adapted) — page 16
The heavens are telling the glory of God.
(Psalm 19:1) — page 18
O taste and see that the LORD is good.
(Psalm 34:8) — page 19
Clap your hands, all you peoples; shout to
God with loud songs of joy. (Psalm
47:1) — page 20
God fills my life with good things. (Psalm
103:5, *Good News Bible*, adapted) — page 22
This is the day that the LORD has made; let
us rejoice and be glad in it. (Psalm
118:24) — page 24
Children are a gift from the LORD. (Psalm
127:3, *Good News Bible*) — page 26
Let everything that breathes praise the
LORD! (Psalm 150:6) — page 27

Isaiah
Do not fear, for God is with you. (Isaiah
41:10, adapted) — page 28

New Testament

Matthew
And remember, I am with you always.
(Matthew 28:20) — page 30

Mark
Blessed is the one who comes in the name
of the Lord! (Mark 11:9) — page 32

John
I am the light of the world. (John 8:12) — page 34

Acts
They all shared with one another. (Acts
4:32, *Good News Bible*) — page 35
Jesus went about doing good. (Acts 10:38,
adapted) — page 36

Romans
Love one another warmly as Christians.
(Romans 12:10, *Good News Bible*) — page 37
Pray at all times. (Romans 12:12, *Good
News Bible*) — page 38

2 Corinthians
God loves a cheerful giver. (2 Corinthians
9:7) — page 39

Galatians
Do good to everyone. (Galatians 6:10, *Good
News Bible*) — page 40

Ephesians
Children, obey your parents. (Ephesians
6:1) — page 41

Philippians
I can do all things through Christ who
strengthens me. (Philippians 4:13,
adapted) — page 42

1 Timothy
For everything created by God is good.
(1 Timothy 4:4) — page 44

Hebrews
Share what you have. (Hebrews 13:16) — page 45

1 John
We are God's children. (1 John 3:2) — page 46